THE ELEPHANT DOCTOR OF INDIA

JANIE CHODOSH

CHICAGO
REVIEW
PRESS

Published by Chicago Review Press Incorporated
814 North Franklin Street
Chicago, Illinois 60610
ISBN 978-1-64160-307-2

Library of Congress Cataloging-in-Publication Data
Library of Congress Control Number: 2020935651

Cover design: Preston Pisellini
Interior design: Jonathan Hahn
All photos courtesy of Dr. Kushal Konwar Sarma

Printed in the United States of America
5 4 3 2 1

Dedicated to the memory of Linnea Mills and to the people of Assam working to coexist with and protect elephants and other wildlife.

Vakratunda Mahakaya Suryakoti Samaprabha
Nirvighnam Kuru Me Deva Sarva-Kaaryeshu Sarvada

O Lord Ganesha of the curved trunk and massive body, the one whose splendor is equal to millions of suns, please bless me so that I do not face any obstacles in my endeavors.

—Hindu mantra

Hindus believe that elephants are the reincarnations of one of their deities, Lord Ganesha. Many Hindu people chant this Sanskrit mantra, or prayer, each morning before beginning their day.

CONTENTS

1 Lakshmi, 1969 ∿ 1

2 Captive Elephants in India:
Mom, Can I Have a Pet Elephant? ∿ 13

3 Elephant School, 1976–1994 ∿ 19

4 Manik, 1994 ∿ 33

5 *Musth* Madness: It's All About the Ladies ∿ 51

6 Govind Singh, 2001 ∿ 59

7 Communication:
My, What Big Ears You Have ∿ 75

8 Lokhimai, 2002 ∿ 81

9 What Does Tea Have to
Do with Elephants? ∿ 95

10 The Wild Bull of Paneri Tea Estate, 2012 ∿ 101

11 Matriarchs and Memory:
Listen to Your Elders ∿ 113

12 Manimala, Alaka, and Shankar, 2015 ∿ 119

13 An Old Friend, 2016 ∿ 135

Afterword: Saving Elephants   145

A Letter from Dr. Sarma   151

Author's Note   155

Facts About Asian Elephants   157

Glossary   161

LaHSHMI
•
1969

Eight-year-old Kushal Konwar Sarma stood by the river that flowed through his small village in Northeast India and watched Lakshmi get a bath. Kushal, or "KK," as his friends and family called him, knew he should be at home studying. He knew his mother would scold him. But he didn't budge. How could he sit with his nose in a book when a few yards from the family compound a full-grown elephant was being bathed?

Rai, the elephant handler, or *mahout* as they're called in India, used a brick to scrub Lakshmi's thick hide, removing dead skin and getting rid of parasites and insects. He then gave her a pedicure, scouring her toenails—five in the front, four in the back—and scraping away calluses. Lakshmi drank in water with her trunk, playfully spraying, trumpeting, and enjoying her bath time. When she emerged from the water, her dark skin gleamed. The freckled pink spots of her ears shone softly in the light.

Rai splashed out of the river after Lakshmi and turned to KK. "Shouldn't you be at home?" he asked.

KK shrugged and inched closer to the elephant. He was so happy to see Lakshmi that he forgot to answer. Instead, he reached out and ran his hand over her bristly and wrinkled skin, not minding that a few stiff hairs poked him and that his hand got wet. Lakshmi flapped her ears and squeaked, as glad to see KK as he was to see her.

KK lived with his parents, three siblings, grandmother, and three uncles and their families. Together they owned over fifty animals, including cows, goats, ducks, pigeons, and dogs. KK loved spending time with all the animals, observing their habits and behavior, helping to feed them and tend to their needs. Elephants, though, were his favorite animals. They were powerful and strong, smart and loyal—like he wanted to be.

As KK stood and admired Lakshmi's great height and strength, he recalled a story that his father, Lankeswar Sarma, had once told him.

"A man named Atma Mahazan was riding his old bull elephant in the countryside when another bull from a nearby village charged the pair and Atma was thrown to the ground," he had said as KK listened, brown eyes wide with wonder. "The bull was in *musth*," his father

continued, explaining that *musth* was a natural condition that happened each year when a male elephant had
a huge rise in the hormone testosterone. This hormonal
change, which prepared the bull for breeding, made the
elephant extremely aggressive. "Atma was hurt, unable
to move, and it looked like the violent bull would kill
him. Knowing his owner was in danger, Atma's elephant
used his trunk to pull the man between his powerful
legs and protect him, all the while fending off the attack
by the angry rival. The old, faithful elephant suffered so
many blows that later he died."

KK had felt sad for the loyal bull when he heard the
story, but he'd also marveled at the way the animal had
sacrificed his life for his owner. On this warm October
day, though, the story soon slipped from his thoughts.
He had just one thing on his mind: spending time with
his 6,000-pound friend. Lakshmi had been living with
his family since spring. Her actual owner, a wealthy
merchant who lived in town and had no place to keep
her when she wasn't working as a logging elephant, had
asked the Sarmas if Lakshmi could stay on their land.

"Can I sit on her while she grazes?" KK asked Rai. It
was a question he asked most days.

Sometimes Rai said yes, sometimes no. Today the
mahout agreed and told the elephant to kneel. KK wasted
no time. Without waiting for Rai to change his mind,
he gently held Lakshmi's ear and climbed onto her left
foreleg. Then, with a small jump, he positioned himself
behind her ears, straddling her strong neck. Once in

place, KK tucked his feet into the rope around Lakshmi's neck.

From so high up, he felt as if he could reach out and touch the hills of Bhutan that painted the northern horizon blue. The hills were 15 miles from his village of Barama in the state of Assam. KK had never before ventured that far from home, but he often wondered what amazing things were hidden there. Little did he know that among the amazing things were the wild elephants that would come to define his life. Each January more than 1,000 elephants, led by the matriarch (the oldest female of the herd), migrated up into the hills to escape the rainy season, returning to the flatlands of Assam in May to birth their calves.

Lakshmi snorted a few times. Then she reached back her trunk to touch KK, a sign of affection, and started to walk. Perched on her neck, bare feet tucked behind her ears, KK felt the muscles of Lakshmi's back ripple. KK gently pressed his right toes forward and guided her toward the sweeter *tara* grasses.

Though the monsoon clouds had disappeared in September, the humidity was still high, and it was hot out, so KK was wearing shorts. His bare legs were an invitation for swarms of biting insects to attack his exposed flesh and the many thorny plants to tear at his legs. He didn't care. A little discomfort was a small price to pay for the precious bit of freedom and time away from studies and chores—but most of all, for time with Lakshmi.

When the boy and the elephant reached the orchard,

Lakshmi grazed on her favorite foods. Besides *tara* grasses, she loved banana stems and bamboo leaves. KK marveled at how she never grew tired of eating. Like all adult elephants, she fed for up to 18 hours a day, consuming 500 pounds of vegetation.

After an hour in the orchard, KK led Lakshmi across the river, watching the silvery bodies of thousands of fish spiraling through the blue. He wanted to show his friend a pair of ground-nesting Indian lapwing birds that were raising their chicks, so he guided her to a nearby bamboo grove. "I'd never show this to my cousins," he confided to the elephant, stroking her sun-warmed head. "I don't trust them not to hurt the birds, but you're so gentle."

Lakshmi, perhaps sensing the compliment, rewarded KK with a squeak, just one of the many sounds she could make. The boy had heard Lakshmi snort, bark, trumpet, and even chirp like a bird. When he sat on her back, he could feel the low rumble she sometimes produced in her chest.

KK found the lapwing nest, and Lakshmi carefully maneuvered her thickly padded feet around the delicate fledglings. The boy and the elephant gazed at the downy gray and white chicks cleverly camouflaged against the river rocks. With his short legs pressed against Lakshmi's muscular shoulders, KK felt a powerful connection to her. He was so lost in the feeling that it wasn't until he heard one of his older cousins calling his name that he shook himself out of his trance.

"Kushal!" his cousin shouted. "Your mother is looking for you. You're in trouble!"

KK sighed. He'd been found out. Besides studying,
he was supposed to be looking after the cows and helping his mother clean, cook, and husk the rice. Most days
he did what was expected of him, but when it came to
Lakshmi, he couldn't help it; sometimes he just over-
looked his responsibilities.

"Our time is over for the day," he told his friend. He
wasn't in much of a hurry, though. He was already in
trouble. No need to rush. He slowly guided the elephant
back to the orchard, taking his time to watch a shim-
mering blue bee-eater dart off its perch, catch a wasp,
then thwack the insect against a branch to pound out its
venom before enjoying a midday snack. Lakshmi also
snacked, tearing at leaves and branches with her trunk as
she walked. Once KK and Lakshmi passed back through
the orchard, Rai woke up from the nap he'd taken after
a lunch of cooked rice and chili.

"Time to study, *Baba*?" the *mahout* asked, addressing
KK the way an employee of an Assamese family typ-
ically addressed a young boy of his age. Rai then told
Lakshmi to kneel.

KK reversed his earlier routine—descending from
the elephant's back, holding on to her ear, and stepping
on her raised left foreleg. "Study and eat," he responded,
suddenly realizing how hungry he was. "But I'll be back
tomorrow!" He reached the ground and said goodbye
to Rai. Then he kissed Lakshmi's trunk and raced up

the path toward the family compound that led past the grove of orange trees.

Besides oranges, his family grew pineapple, mango, jackfruit, coconut, betel nut, sugarcane, peanuts, rice, cauliflower, cabbage, onion, tomato, and eggplant. They also had many varieties of valuable trees, which his paternal grandfather knew how to use for their medicinal properties. Between the farm animals, crops, and trees, the only thing his mother, Giribala Devi, had to buy from the store was salt.

When KK got to the two-room thatched house that he shared with his parents and three siblings, he slowed down and tiptoed inside, hoping to wash before he encountered his mother. Riding Lakshmi was one thing—being covered in dust and dirt, scratches and dried blood, was another. KK was an adventurous child and knew from many previous unsanctioned outings that his mother wouldn't be happy. He made it past the kitchen and the dining room and was almost to the bathroom when his mother saw him.

She took in his ragged appearance and threw her oldest son a hard look. "Where have you been?" she scolded, though KK was sure she knew the answer. "No food? No studies? No chores?" she went on. "Do you want to be a *mahout*? If you continue to do this, I'll ask your papa to send Lakshmi back!"

"Ma, please, I'm sorry. Don't tell *Pita*," KK pleaded with downcast eyes. "I won't do it again." But he knew that wasn't true. The first chance he got, he'd be back with Lakshmi.

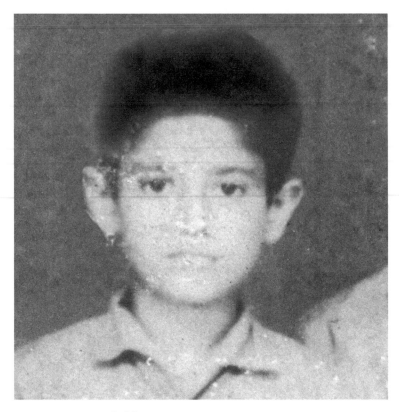

KK as a young child.

And that's exactly what happened.

Over the next year, KK stole as much time as possible with the gentle cow elephant. He snuck to the orchard whenever he had the chance, riding her when he had time, slipping her a treat of rice or a banana when he didn't. Often, *Aba*, his paternal grandmother, came with him. Like KK, his grandmother loved elephants, and she especially loved Lakshmi. Sometimes, she'd bring the elephant a plate of rice and fruit, and then she and her grandson would paint the *tilak* mark, a sign of blessing or greeting made with red vermilion paste, on Lakshmi's forehead.

When KK was nine years old, though, everything changed.

KK's father was a pharmacist. He had a small business about one mile from home, but there were few trained pharmacists in those days, and the government persuaded him to accept a job at the state health department in a new village. KK understood that a new village meant they'd have to move, which meant leaving his cousins, his grandmother, the farm, and all the animals. And of course, it meant leaving Lakshmi. The night his father delivered the news, KK went to his room and cried.

∿

Although he'd been sad to leave, KK quickly adapted to his new life. He made friends with the Bodo tribal children who lived in the area, which was called Borkmakha, and he enjoyed his family's modern government living quarters. Still, he pined for his extended family and for Lakshmi. When his father decided after a year to move the family back to Barama, KK was ecstatic. He prepared to reunite with his grandmother, his cousins, and all the animals, but he was most excited to reunite with Lakshmi.

The day they returned to their village, KK raced to the orchard with a banana for his best friend. He couldn't wait to touch her, to hear her trumpet, to sit up high on her massive back and amble to the river. When he arrived, though, the orchard was empty. Lakshmi was gone, and so was Rai.

KK ran back to the compound, where he found his grandmother perched on a bamboo mat by a mango tree. "Where's Lakshmi, *Aba*?" he asked, plucking a ripe mango from the tree and then sitting beside his grandmother.

"Her owner sent her to the foothills of Bhutan to do some logging," she said, then paused. To KK, it felt like hours that they sat by the tree, looking toward the blue shadow of the eastern Himalayas on the horizon. Finally, his grandmother spoke again, only now her voice sounded strained. "While Lakshmi was there, she got an infection."

KK had seen many of the farm animals get sick and then get better again with the help of a local veterinarian, or sometimes on their own. Just last month when he'd visited, one of the goats had developed boils around its neck. The animal, with its painful lumps, bleated in distress, but the veterinarian came, and the goat recovered.

"Is she OK?" KK asked, peering into his grandmother's eyes, searching for good news—that Lakshmi was OK, and as soon as the logging season ended, she'd return.

But his grandmother shook her head and in a barely audible voice said, "Lakshmi died."

KK stared at his grandmother. His mind could hardly grasp what she'd told him, yet his heart understood. He'd never see Lakshmi again. KK slumped forward, buried his face in his grandmother's lap and sobbed. After many minutes passed and he could finally speak, he had just one question: "If they can save a goat, how come nobody could save her?"

"I don't know," his grandmother admitted, her dark eyes glistening. "You love animals. Maybe someday you'll be an animal doctor, and you can learn to save elephants."

KK wondered if what *Aba* said was true. His sadness was overwhelming, but the thought that maybe someday he could help elephants survive injuries and ailments like infections gave ten-year-old KK hope.

CaPTIVE ELEPHANTS IN INDIA

•

MOM, CAN I HAVE A PET ELEPHANT?

"It's up to us, humankind, to assure better treatment for elephants, man's best friend through the ages."
—Dr. KK Sarma

Chances are you have a dog or a cat or know someone who does. Or maybe you raise backyard chickens or have a horse. These animals are domestic, meaning they have been bred to live with humans.

Take dogs, for example. Our relationship with *Canis familiaris* goes back at least 15,000 years to when dogs were first domesticated from gray wolves. We don't know exactly how humans and dogs first came together, but we do know that dogs are the only large carnivores to have been domesticated. Yep, Snoopy is descended from a wolf.

Elephants might not be carnivores, but they are large. And in the first chapter, you read that young KK had Lakshmi—an elephant—as a friend. She wasn't, however, a pet. She wasn't a domesticated animal, even though she was tame.

Here's why. Most captive elephants in India have been caught directly from the wild, or their parents were. They haven't been bred by humans for generations. Imagine if they had been. Would there be tiny elephants, like the miniscule chihuahua? Spotted elephants, like the dalmatian? Elephants with curly tails? That's what humans do to domestic animals: we breed them to bring out the traits that we want.

The word *captive* implies something negative, typically meaning to be held against one's will. Think of animals in zoos. They're captive. Forget for a minute whether you think zoos are good or bad, right or wrong. You can see the difference between domestic and captive. The animals in zoos aren't pets; they aren't tamed to snuggle or bring in the newspaper. They're wild animals behind bars and fences.

Not all captive elephants in India are in zoos, but they're still kept from returning to the wild by various means, such as hobbles (chains on their front legs). For now, though, put aside thoughts on captivity and we'll focus on the history of these elephants in India, because they've been around for a long time.

Elephants have played an important role in Indian religion, myths, history, and cultural heritage going back thousands of years. Relying on images in rock paintings, some historians trace human-elephant relationships in India all the way back to 6000 BCE. Ancient Indian texts such as the *Rig Veda* (1500–1000 BCE) and the Upanishads (800–500 BCE) have many references to trained elephants. They were also part of nation building and defense. As early as 300 BCE, India's kings and emperors maintained huge armies of elephants for battle. In 326 BCE the ancient Indian king Porus used 130 war elephants to fight against Alexander the Great. Porus lost, and the elephants did with him.

More peacefully, elephants play an important role in some religions. In Hinduism (the religion with the largest following in India), one of the most important gods, Ganesha, has the head of an elephant. In Buddhism, a religion practiced in India and elsewhere, the Buddha himself is linked with an elephant.

In Assam, in particular, elephants are tied closely with culture. The Ahoms, a group of people from Thailand, crossed into the region in the 13th century on a convoy of elephants. The Ahom tradition and knowledge of elephants merged with that of the native peoples—the Moran, Mishsing, Singpho, Khamti, and Rabha—and a unique elephant-keeping culture evolved. Elephants were revered. They were written about and painted.

Then the British took over. (You can read more about this in chapter 9.) They had quite a different relationship with elephants. It wasn't about art or reverence; it was about exploitation of resources. To the British,

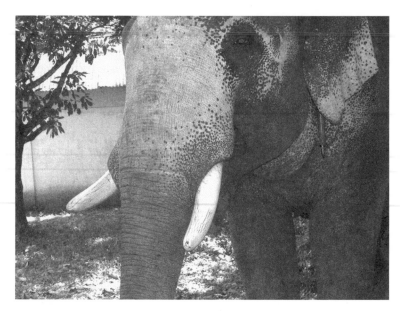

Captive elephants, like this male, have a long history in India.

the elephant was a 10,000-pound bulldozer. They were used to fell trees, to clear forests, to prepare the land for railroads and tea plantations. And when there weren't enough elephants to do the job, they captured more.

Today, there are about 1,260 captive elephants in Assam and 1,490 throughout the rest of India. Some of these animals are owned by the forest department and used in antipoaching patrols and to drive away herds of wild elephants from farms and villages. Their care is overseen by people such as Dr. Sarma. Those that aren't owned by the forest department are owned privately. Some of these elephants are kept isolated in temples and adorned, decorated, and paraded during festivals.

Others are kept in circuses or used to give tourists rides. And not all are treated well. Many are shackled, under-nourished, and treated as a form of entertainment. From a history of being revered, many of these mighty creatures have been reduced to slaves.

Now think about animals in captivity, again. Pause to ask yourself not just what's right, but what rights animals should have. Should elephants be captive? If so, to what degree and under what circumstances? What about other animals? Where do we draw the line?

Domestic, captive, or wild, elephants and all animals are affected by our actions. In America our ball-chasing, tail-wagging dogs might be "man's best friend," but in India, no doubt, that role is played by elephants. As such, these companions in captivity deserve to be treated with love and respect.

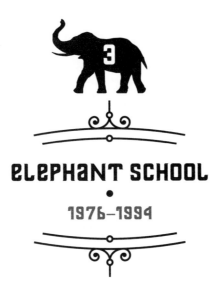

ELEPHANT SCHOOL
•
1976–1994

One year after Lakshmi died, KK sat at his desk in his small bedroom. He lit a kerosene lamp and prepared to study, but he didn't open his books. Instead, he gazed out the window, past the trees toward the orchard where his elephant friend had once lived. Although the ache in his chest had lessened and the sadness had faded into the sweet memories of their friendship, he still missed her.

KK often thought about what his grandmother said on the day he'd learned of Lakshmi's death. He wondered what the future would hold for him. Would he learn to take care of elephants? Sometimes that thought depressed him, for who would teach him such a thing when there wasn't a veterinarian anywhere who knew how to cure an elephant with an infection?

Twilight faded into a dark night sky, and soon the moon rose above the Mora Pagladia, the river where Lakshmi once bathed. As a pack of village dogs barked and someone turned on a radio, KK's mind wandered. Then he heard his bedroom door open and he looked up to see his mother standing in the shadows.

"Daydreaming?" she asked.

He admitted he was and promised he'd get to work. KK loved school, and when his mother left, he opened a book. For two hours he studied by the light of the lamp, immersing himself in geography, math, and history. He was a good student, earning top grades at Deulguri Primary School, and his teachers liked him. KK wanted to go to college someday, but his family didn't have much money. If he wanted to study to be a veterinarian and help elephants, he'd have to do well in school and earn a scholarship.

When he turned 15, his chance to compete for a scholarship arrived. In order to get it, though, he'd have to take a test—along with 100,000 other students across Assam. Out of all those students, the top 10 percent would earn a place at Cotton College, the best college in the state.

The day of the exam, KK's stomach turned with nerves. He didn't want breakfast, but his mother insisted.

"You have to eat something," she said, bringing him boiled rice and some mashed potatoes. KK managed to do as his mother said, and after eating he walked to school to take the exam.

For three hours KK sat on a hard wooden bench at a desk shared with two other students. He focused on numbers and facts, dates and equations. Finally, he finished and handed in the test. He had no idea how he'd done, but that night he kneeled in front of a statue of Lord Ganesha, the Remover of Obstacles, one of the most important deities in his Hindu religion. He prayed to the elephant-headed god that he had done well.

One month later the results came.

Not only had KK done well—his score was among the top 100 in Assam. He'd earned the national scholarship and a seat to Cotton College. Several weeks after receiving the news, KK left Barama for the first time and traveled on his own to Guwahati, the busy capital of Assam, for two years of preuniversity study. He'd never been to the city before. He'd never left home alone. But when he stepped onto the bus, a metal trunk containing all his clothes clasped in his hands and his rolled-up quilt and pillow jammed under his arm, he didn't look back.

∿

Getting accustomed to urban life was hard, as was the lack of guidance. There were many things to distract KK in his first months at Cotton College. His new friends wanted to go to the movies at night instead of studying, and there was always something fun to do instead of schoolwork. But KK quickly realized that studies were his priority, and after two years he graduated with top marks. Now it was time to choose his next course of study and apply to a four-year university.

KK still loved animals, and although he hadn't had a chance to be around elephants since Lakshmi, he hadn't given up his goal of getting a veterinary degree and helping them. There was just one problem: his father wanted him to be a medical doctor and work with people. KK didn't want to disappoint him.

As the date to turn in his application for veterinary school drew closer, KK paced his small dormitory room and fretted over his predicament. The pull to please his family was strong, but his desire to help elephants was even stronger. One night, unable to sleep, he wandered to the library. He sat alone in the back of the room and began looking at books about elephants. In one book, he encountered a section on elephant diseases. As he read through the section, an interesting fact caught his attention.

The larva of an insect called the elephant botfly is common in elephants in the foothills of Bhutan and in the state of Arunachal Pradesh. This larva commonly causes infections that can be deadly to elephants if not treated.

KK couldn't believe what he'd just read. He pushed away the book and rose to his feet. Was this the larva that had caused Lakshmi's infection and killed her? If so, how could this have happened? Botflies were common, yet the veterinarian who'd treated her hadn't recognized the source of infection and therefore hadn't been able to save her. Or could it be that there was no established treatment for infection? How could nobody know how to take proper care of elephants when they had played such an important role in Indian culture? And with so many captive elephants living in Assam, who was giving them the medical attention they needed?

KK knew what he had to do. At age eighteen, he applied to the College of Veterinary Science at Assam Agricultural University, also in Guwahati. Although elephant care wasn't a field, he'd learn everything he could about treating other animals. From there, he'd find a way to work with his favorite creature and to make sure they received the care they deserved.

But first he had to tell his parents.

∿

When the hot, rainy summer arrived after two years at Cotton College, KK traveled back home to Barama. One night the clouds cleared, and KK sat in the courtyard with his father and maternal grandparents. As fireflies flashed, wild jackals snuck from the forest to the backyard for scraps, and the village dogs barked, KK worked up the courage to confess his plans. He cleared his throat and told his father that he had applied to college to be a veterinarian.

His father took his time responding. "If that's what you want to study, then I support you," he eventually said.

"But he'll be injecting and hurting cows!" KK's maternal grandmother exclaimed, horrified at the possibility that as a veterinarian her grandson might harm a cow, a sacred animal to Hindu people. "How can a Brahmin boy do such a thing?" she continued, referring to their high Hindu caste, or class.

"The boy won't be hurting the cows. He'll be helping them," KK's grandfather told his wife. "Besides, treating animals is a noble profession and a family tradition." He explained that their family's ancestors had practiced Ayurvedic healing, a type of herbal medicine that began on the Indian subcontinent over 2,000 years ago. He went on to explain that Ayurvedic practitioners had learned about many of the healing herbs from watching elephants—what bark, leaves, and grasses they chose when they were sick or had a mineral deficiency.

Although KK had never thought of it before, his choices were steering him not just toward elephants but also toward his ancestral heritage.

∿∿

With his family's blessing, KK followed through with his plans and attended veterinary school. When he graduated in 1983, having earned a university gold medal from the governor of Assam for his high marks, KK had another professional choice to make. He was offered a government veterinary job in a rural hospital, working with cows and livestock. The pay was decent, but the job would mean working full-time rather than going back to school for a master's degree, where he could learn more about treating elephants.

Although KK desperately wanted to go for the master's degree, this dream seemed more out of reach than ever. He was twenty-two years old. At some point he'd want to get married and have children. How would he make a living as an elephant doctor? And what about his family at home? He had to think about them, too. As the oldest son and second-oldest child, it was his responsibility to help support the family, and especially to help put his siblings through college.

KK couldn't bear the thought of giving up his dream, but he also couldn't bear the thought of letting down his parents and siblings. What to do next weighed on him more than anything he'd ever had to decide. Elephants or responsibility? Dreams or family? He couldn't see a way to have both.

Finally, he decided. He'd be responsible and accept the job.

∿

KK was in his dorm room filling out the paperwork for the government position when Dr. Jorgen Das, a master's degree student in his final year of study and KK's mentor, came to see him. "I heard about your new job," Dr. Das said.

KK nodded. He didn't want to discuss his decision.

"You were the best student in the class," Dr. Das went on. "You should continue your education and get your master's degree."

KK took a breath and confided his dilemma about his family's finances to his mentor.

"But you're a licensed veterinarian now!" Dr. Das exclaimed. "Why don't you go back to school and, in your off hours, start your own veterinary practice? Having your own practice will pay better than a government job, and I can help you get started."

KK hadn't considered such a bold move. Now that the idea of setting up his own practice had been suggested, though, he wondered if he could really do it. What would be the outcome of such a choice? Would he earn more on his own than working for the government, as Dr. Das had suggested? Would he be able to find enough time to attend classes and study?

KK looked out the window toward the busy street. He thought of Lakshmi and smiled. His decision was made. He'd take the risk.

The day after talking to Dr. Das, KK turned down the government position. Within one month he'd started his own veterinary clinic, largely focusing on helping cows. He also returned to school for a master's degree in veterinary surgery.

Soon KK, now known as Dr. Sarma, was earning more in his practice than he could have in the government job, just as his mentor had predicted. He loved working in the clinic to treat animals and relieve them from their pain.

Everything was going well, except for one thing. In his practice, Dr. Sarma still hadn't found a way to work with elephants, and in school there were hardly any courses on elephant care. Dr. Sarma took what few classes were offered. He sat in the hot, humid lecture halls, taking notes on the basic aspects of treating elephants, such as how to deworm them and how to treat abscesses and logging injuries. But the information was basic, and there was no practical application to what he was learning. Without hands-on experience, his studies were just theory. Dr. Sarma longed to be near elephants, to feel their skin beneath his hands, and to work more with the animals that were his first love.

In 1987 he got his first chance to do just that.

One day Dr. Sarma was walking out of class when Dr. Pathak, his adviser and one of the only elephant veterinarians in India, approached him. "I'm going to Manas National Park tomorrow to treat an elephant named Durgaprasad who has an infected tusk," he said. "Do you want to come with me?"

Dr. Sarma eagerly accepted the invitation. He was excited to travel to the Indo-Bhutan border and visit Manas, a wild region of thick forests, pristine grasslands, and powerful rivers. He was even more excited to meet Durgaprasad.

∿

When Dr. Sarma and Dr. Pathak arrived at Manas the next day after a three-hour journey, the *mahout* took them to see Durgaprasad. Dr. Sarma gasped when he saw the magnificent bull. The elephant must have been ten feet tall, with tusks reaching down low and long on either side of his trunk. His thoughts immediately carried him back to Lakshmi, to the strength and beauty of his childhood friend. He'd seen many elephants since his days with her, but he'd seldom had a chance to be so close to one. He felt humble in the presence of such a noble animal.

"Durgaprasad is our main elephant used for anti-poaching patrols," the *mahout* explained, referring to Durgaprasad's job as a *koonkie*, a captive elephant trained to work.

Dr. Sarma nodded, understanding that many poachers came to India from other countries to kill elephants for their ivory and endangered one-horned rhinos for their horns. He knew that due to the population of Bengal tigers in the park, it wasn't safe for game wardens to patrol on foot. There weren't roads, so driving was also off limits. Besides, a motorized vehicle would make too much noise. The wardens had to be quiet, relying on stealth to track and confront the poachers. Elephants were the perfect companion for the job.

Dr. Sarma longed to touch Durgaprasad, to connect with the elephant for a moment. "Can I get closer to him?" he asked the *mahout*.

The *mahout* shook his head. "It's not safe. You have to take your time with him."

Although he was disappointed, Dr. Sarma respected

the *mahout*'s decision. He stayed ten feet away from the large bull elephant.

Dr. Pathak, however, ignored the *mahout*'s advice. He walked right up to Durgaprasad to begin his examination. "First I'll examine the tusks for any cracks," he said, narrating the procedure, so Dr. Sarma could learn the proper techniques of field care.

Dr. Sarma stood to the side, notebook in hand, and scribbled notes. He didn't want to miss anything. He'd just finished writing down what his professor said when, without warning, Durgaprasad lashed out his trunk and struck at Dr. Pathak, hitting him in the chest and knocking him to the ground.

Dr. Sarma raced over to his professor. "Are you OK?" he asked, keeping one eye on the elephant.

"I'm OK," he said, groaning and accepting Dr. Sarma's outstretched hand. Dr. Pathak rose to his feet and finished examining Durgaprasad and treating the infection, all the while grumbling about the poorly trained elephant.

Despite Dr. Pathak's complaints, Dr. Sarma wasn't convinced that what had just happened was related to Durgaprasad's training. Two thoughts came to his mind.

His first thought was that elephants, like people, had moods. If a veterinarian first assessed an elephant's mood by spending enough time looking at the animal, developing a relationship and communicating with it before simply approaching the patient, he believed there'd be less risk of attack.

Dr. Sarma thought that before Dr. Pathak had approached Durgaprasad he should have tried to gauge the elephant's mental state. If the animal was in a bad mood—which Durgaprasad surely was, with his infected tusk—then the doctor should have used extreme caution. Dr. Sarma also realized that what had just happened to Dr. Pathak wasn't his teacher's fault. The problem was that nobody in India had paid attention to this aspect— or hardly any aspect, for that matter—of elephant care.

Dr. Sarma's second thought was about anesthesia, or the lack of it. If Durgaprasad was dangerous, then perhaps he should have been sedated with anesthesia, a medicine used to numb areas of pain. The animal would then be tranquil before Dr. Pathak approached him. Sedation, however, was out of the question because there was no established method for giving anesthesia to an elephant. Without anesthesia, though, it was impossible to operate on an elephant, and therefore a variety of serious injuries and illnesses went untreated.

Dr. Sarma took another look at Durgaprasad and vowed he'd do something to advance the treatment of elephants. The best way he could help, he decided, would be to develop a technique for administering anesthesia to a 10,000-pound animal. To invent such a radical new practice, he'd have to go back to school. In 1991 Dr. Sarma decided to pursue his PhD and come up with a novel way to give an elephant a shot.

∿

One year into the College of Veterinary Science's doctoral program, KK was making good progress toward his PhD, and his veterinary practice with cows and companion animals was flourishing. But there was one problem: his medical work with elephants was still just theory.

Dr. Sarma wanted to turn his attention more fully to the animals of his childhood, to his beloved memories of Lakshmi and to her kin. He knew that elephants were dying all the time for lack of good medical care. What he wanted most was to save them. But he still didn't know how to make this happen.

In 1994 Dr. Sarma was just finishing his PhD when something unexpected happened that would set the course of his career with elephants in motion.

MANIK
•
1994

On Republic Day, January 26, 1994—the anniversary of the day in 1950 that India officially adopted its constitution and became a republic—people throughout the country were celebrating. But not Dr. Sarma. Instead of joining in the festivities, he was finishing an operation on a Labrador retriever in his busy clinic in Guwahati. He'd just stitched the wound when a blue truck pulled up in front of his office and a young man came to the door.

"My name is Rajesh Goel," the man said with a traditional *namaskar* gesture of greeting, palms together in front of his chest. "I've driven 200 miles to see you."

"How can I help you?" Dr. Sarma asked, taking in the young man's big, dark eyes, long nose, and tall frame.

KK thought he must be a Marwari, a group of desert dwellers from the adjacent regions of Pakistan who had widely migrated across India.

"I've come because of my family's tusker," Rajesh said, referring to a male elephant with tusks, as opposed to a *makhna,* a male elephant that doesn't develop any. "His name is Manik, and my grandfather bought him when the elephant was seven years old. That was twenty years ago. I used to ride him to the river to give him a bath when I was a child," he explained, reminding Dr. Sarma of his own childhood. "For many years, Manik was a faithful companion, and when he became an adult, my uncle started using him as a logging elephant in the foothills of Arunachal Pradesh at a new sawmill in the forests outside the village of Tipi."

Rajesh stopped for breath and Dr. Sarma eyed the clock, thinking of the three other dogs waiting for treatment and wondering where this story was going. But he was always eager to hear about an elephant, so he encouraged Rajesh to continue.

"Everything was fine until last week," Rajesh went on. "Then some heavy rains forced the logging work to stop. The *mahouts* let the elephants loose for grazing. After five days, Manik's *mahout,* Ali, went out to fetch Manik from a nearby bamboo thicket. That's when he noticed that something was seriously wrong."

Dr. Sarma wondered if the elephant had been hurt or if he'd hurt someone. He asked Rajesh to continue, and the young man explained that Manik had lowered his

head with his ears forward and erect. Then he charged
at Ali, who fled.

"Five days of grazing and no work brought him into
musth," Rajesh exclaimed. *"He's* loose above the village!"

Dr. Sarma closed his eyes for a moment, fearing what
was coming next. While in *musth*, a bull's testosterone
level can spike to as much as 60 times greater than usual.
This hormonal change makes a male elephant extremely
aggressive. In the wild, *musth* lasts for about one month,
but in captive elephants *musth* can last for as long as three
months. Sometimes the *mahout* isn't ready or properly
trained to observe the signs of the condition, such as a secretion called temporin that flows from openings between the
bull's eyes and ears and stains his cheeks. Once *musth* sets
in, the bull might break loose from his hobbles and take
out his aggression on a house, a truck, or even a person.

"Has anyone been hurt?" asked Dr. Sarma, running
his fingers across his thick black mustache. He was
thinking about how just the previous week a *musth* bull
in a nearby village had attacked and killed his *mahout*
along with several villagers. The government declared
the animal a rogue—a solitary elephant that has become
dangerous and unpredictably violent—and he'd been
killed. The deaths of the people and the death of the elephant weighed heavily on his mind.

"Nobody's been hurt," Rajesh said. "Not yet. But
Manik is still loose and the villagers are terrified."

"And the *mahout?*" asked Dr. Sarma. "How did he
escape?"

Rajesh described how Ali had managed to climb a tree where he had to stay until late at night because Manik wouldn't leave. "When the elephant finally disappeared into the forest, Ali slid down the tree and stumbled through the darkness to the sawmill. When he arrived, it was just getting light, and he told the people camped there, including Rajesh's uncle, what had happened."

The mid-morning sun warmed the chilly office. Dr. Sarma listened to the sound of traffic, the honking truck horns, and the shouts from the drivers of the brightly painted three-wheeled rickshaws. "What about Manik?" he asked, imagining the frightened villagers and the elephant charging through the forest. "Where is he now?"

Rajesh clasped his hands together and paced the office. "One of the people camped on the stream bank by the sawmill suggested they use some *koonkies* to capture Manik and bring him back to the safety of his *mahout*, where he could be tended to and nobody would get hurt. Ali got three *koonkies*, two females and a *makhna* named Golap, and they headed back up into the hills."

Dr. Sarma shook his head, thinking they hadn't done the right thing, but he encouraged Rajesh to tell the rest of the story.

"When the three elephants and their *mahouts* found Manik, he charged Golap and gored him," Rajesh said. "The two female *koonkies* ran off, and the team had to retreat."

Dr. Sarma exhaled and got up to make some tea and tell the owners of the dogs waiting for treatment that he'd be with them shortly. Even without Rajesh telling him the outcome of this story, he feared what would happen next: Manik would be declared a rogue. A tribal councillor, pressured by the sawmill owners and citizens of the town, would then give the order to have him killed—if it hadn't happened already.

Dr. Sarma felt helpless. Every elephant was precious to him. He wanted to help these noble animals, not hear about them being shot. But then he realized something: if Manik had already been shot, Rajesh wouldn't be here. "The elephant, what happened to him?" he asked, splashing his tea as he set it down.

"At first the chief wildlife warden of Arunachal Pradesh wasn't able to pass the order to have Manik killed, since the elephant was registered in a different state and hadn't hurt anyone," Rajesh said. "But at 7:30 this morning the order went through. There are already hunters in Tipi. Manik has two days before they kill him."

Dr. Sarma sank into a chair and sighed. "Then how can I help you?" he asked, hearing the sadness in his own voice. "I'm a veterinarian and I care for all animals, but I'm not sure what I can do to help Manik."

Rajesh explained that he'd seen a *National Geographic* video and learned it might be possible to chemically restrain a wild animal using a dart loaded with a sleep-inducing drug. "The second I got to Guwahati, I went straight to the zoo and met the director to ask about this technique. He said it's never been used in

Assam, but that you were studying elephant anesthesia for your PhD and you might be able to help." He paused and looked Dr. Sarma in the eye. "You're Manik's only chance. Will you come?"

Dr. Sarma took his time responding as he contemplated what Rajesh was asking him to do. As Mr. Bonal, the zoo director, had told Rajesh, nobody in Assam had ever used this technique before. The only knowledge Dr. Sarma had of the method was through a video he'd seen in 1990 during the Congress of the Indian Society for Veterinary Surgery in Kolkata. Chemically restraining a dangerous elephant could get him killed. What if he failed? Others could be killed, too. So much was at risk.

"Let me finish with the dogs that are waiting," Dr. Sarma finally said, knowing he couldn't let an elephant down. "Then I'll close early and help you."

∿∿

As soon as his canine patients were taken care of, Dr. Sarma rushed to the zoo with Rajesh. He knew that a remote injection set used for darting wild animals had been laying around there for many years. What he didn't know was whether it would work.

Mr. Bonal greeted Dr. Sarma when he arrived and led him and Rajesh to the room where the equipment was stored. He unlocked a cabinet and pulled out a rusty syringe projector—a device that looked more like a gun than a tool to save an elephant. "Let me get it cleaned and oiled for you," the zoo director said when Dr. Sarma frowned at the projector's broken-down appearance.

While a guard took the projector to clean it, Dr. Sarma rifled through the rest of the boxes. To his surprise, almost everything he needed was there. He gathered two metal syringe barrels, feathered flight directors, rubber plungers, syringe charges for five-milliliter darts, long- and short-range cartridges, and a stock of Immobilon, the drug he'd use to try to chemically restrain Manik. Large-sized pushing needles, known as elephant cannulas, weren't available. He'd have to improvise and make do with smaller needles more suitable for use in rhinos.

The guard returned with the projector and handed it to Dr. Sarma; it looked shiny and almost new. Dr. Sarma nodded. "Let's see how it works." He filled a syringe with some water and fitted it with a charge, a blank explosive cartridge used inside the syringe to push the drug inside the body of the animal. The four men went outside, and Dr. Sarma loaded the syringe into the projector and shot at a plantain tree to test the equipment.

The syringe struck the target, but when Dr. Sarma pulled it from the tree, he was dismayed by what he found. Although the syringe had been discharged, it didn't release the water, or what would be the medicine, into the target, which would be the elephant. "Not to worry," he said, catching the nervous glances of the other men. Dr. Sarma tried three more times, but the syringe refused to work. Now he was frustrated. Every stalled moment brought Manik closer to death.

"What now?" Rajesh said, eyes wide.

Dr. Sarma sensed the young man's panic. He thought about the faulty device, guessing at what might make it work. "We need fresh syringe charges," he said, feigning complete confidence in the idea.

Rajesh looked at Mr. Bonal. "Where do we get them?"

The director sighed. "There aren't any in the zoo, and as far as I know, none in Assam."

"They have to be available somewhere in India," Dr. Sarma insisted. Now that he'd agreed to the mission, he was determined to carry it out. Then he remembered the address of a supplier he'd heard about when he first learned about this method in 1990. "We can get them in New Delhi," he announced.

"But that's 1,200 miles away," Rajesh protested. "Three hours by plane."

"Then let's book a ticket," said Dr. Sarma.

∿∿

At 5:00 that evening, Rajesh, who'd agreed to fly to the capital and get the supplies, arrived back in Guwahati with the new syringe charges. Dr. Sarma tested the equipment and was thrilled and relieved to find that it worked. He loaded the lorry, or truck, with the jute ropes and chains he'd need to tether Manik—assuming he could indeed sedate and capture the elephant. By 7:30 he and Rajesh set off for Tipi.

Dr. Sarma loads a tranquilizing gun as he prepares to go save an elephant.

As Dr. Sarma drove over the bridge that crossed the Brahmaputra River, the largest river in Assam, he started to worry. He didn't have a firearm. He wasn't a good tree climber, but he'd have to climb a tree in order to dart the elephant. And the drug he was about to use was an opiate narcotic, a very dangerous drug and highly toxic to humans. To make matters worse, Dr. Sarma feared that the hunters, eager to collect both the government bounty and the ivory, would go ahead and kill Manik.

With these worries in mind, Dr. Sarma didn't speak much to Rajesh, who, at 11:30 suggested they stop for the night and rest. Although Dr. Sarma was eager to reach their destination, he agreed. There was nothing he and Rajesh could do to help Manik in the dark. Plus, he was exhausted, and the unpaved roads were too rough and dangerous to complete the journey that night.

After a restless night's sleep on cots at a camp by a railway station, Dr. Sarma and Rajesh awoke early and continued their journey. At 7:30 they reached the town of Balipara, where Rajesh's uncle lived.

Rajesh's uncle welcomed them into his house and led the pair into the sitting room where a group of wealthy Marwari timber merchants were seated. The men had come for two reasons: Manik and a string of kidnappings. The combination of the rogue lurking in the forest and tribal militants in the area who'd kidnapped three people had brought business to a halt.

"Can you capture the elephant?" one of the men asked.

Dr. Sarma noticed the way the man looked him up and down with a scowl. Another man gave him a similar disdainful look. He swallowed, understanding that the merchants had expected a fierce and grizzled-looking elephant hunter, not a young man with an optimistic smile and a love for animals. Before he could answer, though, another merchant spoke.

"Why waste time trying to capture him? The elephant should be killed right away. It's what we've always done before when we had a problem."

"I brought Dr. Sarma here so we could try something

new and try to save Manik," Rajesh's uncle said, a pleading look in his eyes.

Dr. Sarma understood the look. Although it had been many years, he could still recall the love he felt for Lakshmi. He knew Rajesh's uncle felt the same for Manik. Dr. Sarma wanted desperately to save Manik's life. Although he had no idea if he could do it, he ignored the contemptuous looks of the merchants and promised he'd try.

Another man started to speak, but Rajesh's uncle ushered Dr. Sarma and Rajesh from the room. "Have some breakfast and then get going quickly," he told them once they were out of earshot of the others. "These men want Manik killed. You don't have much time." He fed them some rice and tea, gave directions to the sawmill, and sent them on their way.

∿

The lorry bumped and rattled along the rutted roads, snaking through the forested foothills of the Himalayas. With each jounce of the vehicle, Dr. Sarma felt as if his organs would be knocked loose. Finally, they arrived at the sawmill at 10:30 AM, where a thin man in a khaki forest-warden uniform was waiting for them.

Dr. Sarma climbed out of the lorry, got his syringe projector, and greeted the man. But as he introduced himself, he wasn't looking at the warden. He was looking at the two tribal hunters standing beside him. The hunters, dressed in *dhotis*, layered cloth draped around their waists, each carried a rifle. They puffed locally made cigarettes and smirked at Dr. Sarma.

His stomach tightened, but he tried to ignore their condescending looks. He assumed the men were pleased to see that he had such a primitive tool, one that looked more like something for hunting birds than for capturing an elephant. He suspected the hunters felt assured of their own successful hunt and the monetary reward they'd get from the government, plus the ivory. He told himself not to worry, that his weapon could subdue and save Manik.

"Ali and several villagers are camped high in the hills close to where Manik was last spotted," the warden said. "If Manik hasn't been restrained by the end of the day, I'll have to send out the hunters." With a serious look and a solid shake of Dr. Sarma's hand, he pointed them toward the camp. "Good luck," he said. "Be careful. The elephant is dangerous."

Dr. Sarma thanked him. With a final glance at the hunters, he and Rajesh hurried on. As they climbed higher into the mountains, the road trailed off into an eroded dirt path strewn with boulders and cratered by potholes. Progress became painfully slow; it took them over half an hour to drive just two miles.

Finally, they reached the camp on a high ridge surrounded by hills that the warden had described. Smoke rose from a campfire. A half-cooked pot of rice smoldered on the logs. Plastic plates lay scattered on the ground. But nobody was around. Even the birds had stopped singing. Dr. Sarma and Rajesh exchanged nervous glances.

"Why is it so quiet?" Rajesh whispered.

"I don't know. Wait here. I'll go investigate."

Dr. Sarma stepped out of the vehicle and slowly walked toward the campfire. "Hello!" he called into the silence. "My name is Dr. Sarma. I've come to try to capture Manik."

Seconds later someone called back. Dr. Sarma looked uphill in the direction of the voice and saw five men huddled together on a big rock. A small man wrapped in a blanket waved for him to approach. Dr. Sarma trudged up the hill, breathing heavily with the thin air of the higher altitude.

When he got to the rock, the man in the blanket stood up. "My name is Ali. I'm Manik's *mahout*. The other men here are from the village," he said.

"What happened?" Dr. Sarma asked, glancing back toward the abandoned campfire.

Ali squatted and pulled the blanket tighter around his shoulders. "Manik appeared while we were cooking. He was aggressive and charged at us. We barely managed to run away to safety." He paused and pointed to the tall *ulu* grass across a creek. "We haven't been able to leave because he's still there."

Dr. Sarma looked at the low hill dotted with slender trees and tall grasses. At the far edge of the hill, the gray hump of an elephant's back peeked out above the grass. Never before had he been so close to a dangerous tusker.

He was scared but quickly pushed away his fear. He had to focus. He had just hours before the professional hunters came for Manik and killed him. He was the elephant's only chance.

Dr. Sarma took a breath and peered from the elephant to the trees. He'd have to climb one if he wanted any chance of darting Manik, but again, he worried about his poor tree-climbing skills.

He knew what he had to do and turned back to Ali. "I need someone to climb a tree," he told the *mahout*. "Someone who can fire a tranquilizing gun."

"I can do it," one of the young men perched on the rock said. He rose and introduced himself as Phuleswar.

Dr. Sarma took in the young man's stocky chest, strong legs, and confident dark eyes and decided he was the one for the job. "Come with me," he said, and led Phuleswar back to the lorry. Dr. Sarma loaded the syringe with the drug, not allowing the biting insects to slow him down or disrupt his concentration. He placed the syringe into the gun, gave the gun to Phuleswar, and explained how to use it. "Make sure there aren't any branches or leaves in your way when you fire," he told Phuleswar. "And make sure you shoot only when Manik is within 100 feet."

Phuleswar nodded. If the young man was nervous, he showed no sign of it. Dr. Sarma then sketched a diagram and showed him the target site on Manik's body. "Aim for the soft tissue around the elephant's rump," he said. "But if Manik is right below you, aim for the side of his spine."

As he spoke, Dr. Sarma ignored his unease over all

the things that could go wrong as he made the final plan. Phuleswar, he decided, would sit on the branch of an *ou*, or elephant apple, an evergreen tree whose fruits were a favorite of elephants. Ali would go a bit farther and climb another tree. When the *mahout* was in place, he'd call Manik's name and lure him in. Dr. Sarma would be hiding behind a boulder with the ropes and chains, so when the tranquilizing medicine took effect he could quickly dash out and tether the elephant.

The plan set, the three men took their places.

Dr. Sarma crouched behind the boulder. His heart hammered as he peered around the side of the big rock and saw the elephant's back still sticking out above the grass. But he was ready. He gave the thumbs up to Ali, who started to call Manik's name.

Phuleswar joined in, chanting, "Manik! Manik!"

The huge elephant stopped eating. He looked at them. Then, with ears erect, Manik galloped furiously toward the tree where Phuleswar was perched in the crook of two skinny branches. Manik roared twice and kept his forward momentum.

If the elephant hit the tree, Phuleswar would be thrown out and crushed.

Before Dr. Sarma could warn him of the impending danger, Phuleswar reached into a cotton bag and heaved a handful of *bheem kal* fruits, a variety of sweet banana and a favorite of captive elephants, to the ground.

Thirty feet from the tree, Manik slowed and stopped to eat.

Phuleswar wasted no time. He fired the syringe from the projector.

The syringe hit Manik in the rump, but the elephant just stood there flapping his ears, swishing his tail, and helping himself to more fruit. Except for his wet cheeks, stained with temporin, Manik looked like a normal elephant.

A minute passed, then another. Dr. Sarma repeatedly eyed his wristwatch. The tusker should've shown signs of sedation in five minutes. Seven minutes had passed, but Manik remained alert. Questions flooded his mind. Had the drug stock lost its potency? Was the needle in deep enough?

And then it happened—the result Dr. Sarma had been waiting for. Manik's trunk went limp. His tail stopped swishing. His ears stopped flapping. Dr. Sarma picked up a pebble and tossed it at the elephant's backside. Manik didn't react.

Thinking the situation safe, Dr. Sarma shouldered his equipment and cautiously crept out from behind the boulder. If he'd been mistaken and Manik wasn't sedated, the elephant could charge and he could be killed.

Dr. Sarma tiptoed across the grass, his breath a tight knot in his chest. Slowly he approached the elephant. Finally, he drew close enough to touch Manik. He leaned forward and saw that Manik's eyes were closed. Though still standing, he was snoring.

"He's sedated!" Dr. Sarma shouted to Rajesh and Ali.

He had no time to waste. The first thing he had to

do was secure Manik, so the tusker couldn't escape or hurt anyone. Dr. Sarma dropped to his knees and hobbled the elephant's front legs together with the ropes and chains he'd brought. His hands trembled as he gazed up from the ground at Manik's massive torso, admiring the power and grace contained within one being.

Dr. Sarma then stood and pulled the syringe from Manik's back. As he did, he discovered why it had taken Manik so long to become sedated.

"Only half the medicine was released," he told Ali, who'd raced to Manik's side the second it was safe.

Dr. Sarma then reached into his bag for a needle and syringe filled with Revivon, a drug used to bring Manik out of sleep. He held out the elephant's ear and injected the medicine into an artery. "You'll have to avoid giving him extra grains and only allow him to forage," he told Ali, instructing the *mahout* on the proper diet and medications to bring down the tusker's testosterone levels.

As Dr. Sarma finished explaining Manik's care to Ali, Rajesh joined the men, carrying with him a bag of sweets he'd brought in from New Delhi. "I was hoping we'd have a reason to celebrate," he said, offering the bag to Dr. Sarma, as Manik opened his eyes.

Dr. Sarma thanked Rajesh and took several treats for himself, then offered one to Manik. The elephant used his trunk to pluck one of the sweets from the doctor's hand. Then, without warning, he lashed out and swatted him.

Dr. Sarma immediately realized his mistake in getting too friendly with the *musth* bull. He lurched backward

Darting and immobilizing a wild elephant in *musth* is dangerous.

to get out of Manik's way, tripping on a root as he did and tumbling to the ground.

"Are you OK?" Rajesh exclaimed, rushing to Dr. Sarma's side and offering his hand.

But Dr. Sarma didn't reach for the outstretched hand, and he didn't answer. Overjoyed at having saved Manik, he just lay on the grass and started to laugh. The others might have thought he was crazy, but he didn't care.

With the late day sun blazing down, Dr. Sarma stared up at the sky with more pride than he'd ever before felt. Not only had he saved Manik's life, but he'd become the first man in Assam to chemically sedate a wild elephant.

His grandmother's words had finally come true. He had saved an elephant.

MUSTH MADNESS
•
IT'S ALL ABOUT THE LADIES

"No animal in the world is as dangerous as an elephant in musth.*"*
—Charles Darwin, 1871

You've probably seen images of a colorful male peacock (or even seen one in person) with his blue and green tail feathers arched into an enormous fan. Or maybe you've seen a *National Geographic* episode of two male musk oxen butting horns.

Throughout the animal kingdom, males have evolved an amazing assortment of showy, macho, and outright strange behaviors. Take the birds of paradise, for example. The dudes of this fanciful avian family have brightly colored streamers, quills, ribbons, and ruffs to rival a Dr. Seuss character. And, as if their feathers weren't extravagant enough, they strut, hang upside down, buzz, trill, dance, hop, waggle, and seem to shape-shift before your very eyes in an effort to dazzle. Lizards do push-ups. Songbirds sing until it seems they will lose their voices. Fairy wrens offer pink petals to those they are courting (pink compliments their iridescent blue cheek feathers). Long-tailed dance flies present their potential mates with juicy insect snacks.

What do all these things have to do with *musth*? One thing. Male competition for a precious limited resource: females.

The guys who get the girls pass on their genes, so in the animal kingdom (of which, don't forget, we are part), the males want the females, and they will go to great lengths to impress them. For elephants, their most macho, female-luring behavior occurs during *musth*.

Musth, from the Hindi word meaning "intoxicated," happens when a young, healthy male elephant, called a bull, gets a big surge of testosterone, the male sex hormone that gives human males more armpit hair and deeper voices, among other things. In male elephants, testosterone makes them desperate to challenge other bulls in a fight for females. Scientists have found testosterone levels in some bull elephants to be more than sixty times higher than when the same elephants are not in *musth*. That's a lot of testosterone flowing through the young guy's blood and making him, well, really desperate to spread his genes.

Musth is natural. Just like boys become men and girls

become women, baby boy elephants become big bull elephants, and as such, they will challenge other big bull elephants for females. This process is healthy. This process helps keep the elephant population growing, ensures the strongest elephants pass on their advantageous genes, and all in all, keeps the pachyderms happy and vigorous.

The problem starts when elephants come into contact with humans—which is happening more and more often. As human population grows . . . and grows . . . and grows . . . where are all the people supposed to live? Many move into forests. In Assam forests are shrinking all the time. And it isn't just the growing human population that reduces them. It is the worldwide demand for products like Yogi's Refreshing Mint, Trader Joe's Spiced Chai, the Republic of Tea's Assam Breakfast—all made with the dark, malty black tea grown in this region on land where forest once stood.

Elephants have excellent memories. Can you remember what happened when you were two or three? Can you remember the paths you walked, the places you visited? Elephants can remember. In fact, they are thought to carry not just their own memories but also those of their ancestors. In northeastern India, elephants migrate between the hills of Bhutan and the valleys of Assam. Led by a matriarch, or elder female, these elephants have been making this journey for thousands of years. The problem is what was once a habitat filled with bamboo forests and some 300 species of plants that elephants love to eat is now either tea plantation or paddy fields. At four tons, an elephant has to eat between 300 and 500 pounds of food a day in order to survive. What's a hungry elephant to do?

Much of the conflict between elephants and humans is about land—who gets it. Sometimes the humans and elephants can work out their disagreements, but during *musth,* things get tricky.

All that testosterone makes a *musth* elephant very aggressive. In the wild this aggression serves a purpose. If the elephant is not in the wild—say he's trapped in a landscape of farms and tea plantations—and he's in *musth,* he's just as aggressive, only now he might take out his aggression on humans. It is important that *mahouts* recognize the signs of the condition.

What are the signs of an elephant in *musth?*

One of the main physical symptoms of *musth* is the oozing of a powerful-smelling liquid from glands between the elephant's eyes and ears. These glands, called temporal glands, are about the size of a human fist and weigh up to one and a half pounds in males.

The important thing, though, isn't the glands themselves but what comes out of them. The ooze that flows from the temporal glands is called temporal gland secretion (TGS) or temporin. Temporin is made of proteins (the things your parents tell you to eat more of, as well as the building blocks of all the tissue in our bodies, including hair, nails, skin and muscle), lipids (fats or similar greasy things that share the characteristic of not dissolving in water), and other compounds, the most important of which is testosterone.

In old Sanskrit (an ancient religious and spiritual Indian language) texts, temporin is referred to as "rut fluid." Rut and *musth* go hand in hand, rut being the time when two males of a species bash horns, beat chests, bump bodies, lock antlers, and otherwise try to dominate one another. In these very old texts, temporin is considered to be a symbol of strength and vigor. In parts of Assam, villagers refer to temporin as *kamsindur*. Some believe that if the *kamsindur* is applied to the woman of one's choice by rubbing it on any part of her body, she will fall madly in love with you.

Temporin was also traditionally considered an antidote for poison, an antiseptic, and a tonic for hair growth. Some ancient traditions even mistook the temporin found in elephants' skulls for pearls.

But what about the elephant? How does the temporin affect him? Besides making him a fighting machine and love vessel, the flow of temporin is painful and probably contributes to his bad temper. The fluid runs down into his mouth. His glands swell, and the swelling causes the glands to press against his eyes. Scientists have even observed *musth* elephants digging their tusks into the ground or pressing their forehead against a tree in an effort, it appears, to ease their pain.

We know what the temporin does to the gentlemen, then, but how does it affect the ladies? Pheromones, special chemicals that smell really good to others of the same species and attract the opposite sex, are also in *musth* fluid. If testosterone is the instigator of the bulls' mating behavior, pheromones are the attractor. A wild bull elephant can often be observed rubbing his cheeks on trees and waving his ears to spread the scent, letting all available females know that he is THE MAN and he is very available.

Besides their exceptional memory, elephants have excellent olfactory perception—a really great ability to smell stuff—as good as or even better than bloodhounds. Females can smell the *musth* secretions when they are just starting, and other males can too, which is a good thing. A male elephant that smells the *musth* secretions of another male elephant might not actually go into *musth* at the same time. In other words, *musth* in one bull suppresses *musth* in another. If two *musth* males do come into contact, however, they will fight until one of them dies or is driven away. The defeated male may turn into a rogue and vent his fury on others—potentially including humans.

In Assam the habitat for elephants has gotten smaller and smaller, while at the same time, the human population has grown larger and larger. An elephant in *musth* is primed to mate, and he will fight other bull elephants and possibly destroy things, both nonliving and living.

Consider this scenario as an example. A *musth* elephant has wandered out of the forest because there isn't enough forest left to meet his home range requirements of about 250 square miles. He wanders into a tea garden.

Dr. Sarma examines a tranquilizing dart.

He's hungry because tea gardens don't offer palatable food for elephants. He's hot because there's not enough shade in a tea garden. He's thirsty because the water, polluted with pesticides, tastes bad. He wanders out of the tea garden, now even more irritable than before. (Wouldn't you be if you hadn't eaten, drank, or rested all day?) He comes to a house, a small dwelling with thatched walls. Perhaps someone in this home has made a type of drink called country brew, an alcoholic beverage with a strong odor, of which elephants are very fond. (Remember their excellent sense of smell?) Mr. Musth, who is hungry, thirsty, tired, pumped with testosterone, and weighs four to five tons, wants in on the goods. Using his size to his advantage, he takes it. How? By trampling the house and, sometimes, those in it.

Across the world, native people have traditional knowledge of the land, of natural medicines, and of cures to help with many things from treating disease to treating *musth* elephants. In Assam elephant handlers of the past had considerable knowledge about *musth* in elephants and could avert disastrous situations by correctly identifying the signs and applying herbal remedies. Mention of such traditional preparations can be found in a 2,000-year-old document called *Gajashastra*, the elephant-scripture handbook. Today, however, most modern *mahouts* have lost this knowledge.

The loss of the traditional knowledge is one reason Dr. Sarma's technique is so important. If it were not for his chemical immobilization, many of these elephants would be shot and many more would likely find their way into homes and cause a lot of harm.

GOVIND SINGH
•
2001

Word of Dr. Sarma's revolutionary success with Manik spread. Soon he was getting calls from forest department wardens, private elephant owners, and frightened villagers from all over northeastern India. He was called when Mohan, a massive *makhna* in *musth* that had killed seven people in the town of Pengeri, was roaming loose. He was called when Lakhiprasad, a towering nine-foot tusker, attacked a truck filled with goods and passengers and turned it upside down, killing the driver. He was called to help a wild tusker in Bengal suffering from a gunshot wound. He was called to save elephants from people and people from elephants. He got call after and call, each begging him to come and save an elephant or save villagers—and each time requiring Dr. Sarma to put his own life at risk.

At times Dr. Sarma tracked elephants on foot, trekking 10 to 12 hours through dense forests. Other times he rode on the back of a *koonkie*. There were many times he narrowly escaped being trampled by a charging elephant—once he even got away from an angry bull by jumping into an icy river and swimming away.

Dr. Sarma married in 1990. He had a son, Sashanka Sekhar ("Bubu"), in 1991 and a daughter, Nirmali ("Nina"), in 1994. He became a professor in the department of surgery and radiology at his alma mater in 1996, all the while maintaining his veterinary practice. But during it all, Dr. Sarma continued his work tracking and saving elephants. His wife worried about his safety, and Dr. Sarma missed his family when he was gone. But he couldn't stop his work. He felt blessed by a strong body, a sense of adventure, and most of all with a love of elephants. If he didn't save them, who would?

∿

In November 2001, Dr. Sarma got a call that would again change his life. He had just finished teaching his last class of the day, and he was in his office reading an article in the local paper. The article explained how several poachers with a truck filled with elephant meat and ivory had been nabbed in the state of Meghalaya, a rugged mountainous region in northeastern India whose name means "abode of the clouds" in Sanskrit. Dr. Sarma felt deep anguish as he read the article. He was thinking about the price of human greed and wondering how anyone could end the life of such an emotional, intelligent, and endangered animal when the phone rang.

He picked up and heard the voice of his brother-in-law, Narayan, a fellow elephant lover and a forest ranger at a national park in northeast Assam, bordering China. Dr. Sarma was happy to talk to his brother-in-law, thinking they'd have a nice chat about their families. Instead, Narayan told him that a captive *makhna* called Govind Singh had escaped and gone on a rampage.

"How many dead?" Dr. Sarma asked, understanding that when an elephant went on a rampage people were usually killed.

"Fourteen," Narayan said quietly.

Dr. Sarma's eyebrows shot up. Fourteen people killed? Surely the animal was in *musth*, but such a high number of fatalities was beyond anything he'd ever heard.

"The *mahout* didn't recognize the signs of *musth*, and by the time he did, it was too late to tether the bull to a sturdy tree," Narayan continued. "Govind Singh killed his *mahout* and his owner. Then he tried to go back to his home after a few days, but the villagers along the way were so scared that they shot at him. That's when he killed the others and disappeared into the forest."

Narayan sighed, and Dr. Sarma could hear his brother-in-law's sadness. The pain he must be feeling was easy to imagine; they both shared a deep love for all creatures, especially elephants.

"Where exactly did this happen?" Dr. Sarma asked.

"In the Nalani Forest Reserve. Three hours' travel from where I am."

Dr. Sarma knew a bit about the landscape in that part of Assam. Most of the land had been cleared for tea plantations, but there were still some remote tracts of forests. These forests were wild and untouched, thick with vegetation and lacking paths and roads.

"Can you come and try to subdue him?" Narayan asked.

"It will be hard to find him in such a rugged landscape." Dr. Sarma looked at the article about the poachers again, then took a breath and added, "Hard, but not impossible. How much time do we have?"

"Tomorrow the chief wildlife warden will sign the order to have him killed."

∿

After washing the darts and other accessories with soap and water and lubricating them with petroleum jelly, Dr. Sarma packed and prepared to leave. Tinsukia, the nearest town to the park where his brother-in-law lived, was about 400 miles from Guwahati. He was too tired to drive that far in one night, so he decided to take an overnight bus and booked a ticket for the 12 hours of travel. He departed Guwahati at eight o'clock that night, and after sleeping through the journey, awoke the next morning at his destination. A forest department warden met him at the bus station and drove him to the ranger station guesthouse, where Narayan greeted them.

Dr. Sarma embraced his brother-in-law, and the two spoke of their children and wives. Once they had caught up on family news, their talk quickly turned to the rogue.

"We have to be cautious and careful not to get too close to him," Dr. Sarma explained as they sat down to a breakfast of chapati and dal. "A dart can't save us from a charging bull at close range." As with the many other bulls that he'd now subdued and saved, Dr. Sarma would have to be clever. He took a bite of green lentils and contemplated the situation. "I think it's best to try to call him in rather than pursue him. We'll use his *musth* to our advantage and lure him in with a female."

Narayan nodded. "I'll call the local forest warden in the area and have him hire a *mahout* and a female *koonkie* for the task."

The call made, the plan set, and breakfast finished, the men set out for the long drive to the forest reserve. It was the dry season and the car kicked up clouds of dust as they traveled through tea plantations.

Mile after mile of glossy green tea plants covered the land. Women in brightly colored saris with woven baskets strapped to their backs worked the rows, picking the fragile leaves.

Dr. Sarma felt sad thinking how this land had once belonged to the elephants, how herds of them still spent days in these plantations when they migrated down from the hills of Bhutan or Arunachal Pradesh. There was nothing for the hungry and thirsty animals to eat or drink in the plantations, but they had nowhere else to go. The forests they used to share with tigers, leopards, and countless other species were disappearing.

Three hours after setting out, they reached the Nalani Forest Reserve, one of the few forest fragments in the area that hadn't been cleared for cultivation. With its thick canopy of titasapa and hollong trees and its tangles of vines and dense undergrowth, the forest was a sharp contrast to the orderly rows of tea plants. Dr. Sarma peered at the wall of vegetation, wondering where Govind Singh had gone and if they'd be able to find him before it was too late.

As the sun beat down, he prepared his equipment, shouldering the syringe projector and slipping into boots. A peacock burst from his roost in a tall tree, trumpeting his *kee-ow, kee-ow* call, his long iridescent feathers trailing like a silk scarf. The pleasant day seemed more suited for a picnic than for tracking a dangerous elephant, but the syringe projector in his hand reminded Dr. Sarma why he was there.

Kutum, the *mahout* Narayan had called, soon joined them with his *koonkie*. Dr. Sarma stroked the elephant as he introduced himself. "We'll stay at the edge of the forest where it's safer and call to Govind Singh from there," he said, knowing that captive *musth* bulls usually responded to their name. "Hopefully the *makhna* will smell the female and come when we call him."

Kutum agreed to the plan. He then stood on his *koonkie*'s strong trunk, which acted as a forklift, carrying him to his perch on her neck. As Dr. Sarma watched the agile *mahout*, he again recalled his days with Lakshmi. Although he'd helped many elephants since then, he hadn't had a bond with one since his childhood friend. He envied the connection between the *mahout* and the elephant.

"Come," Dr. Sarma said, once Kutum was settled on the *koonkie*. He hoisted the syringe projector onto his shoulder and led the team to the forest edge.

"Govind Singh!" they called, as they trudged through tall grasses and skirted around scraggly trees. Sharp spines tore at their pants. Biting ants found their way into their boots. Insects harassed their sweaty foreheads. They called and called until their exhausted voices could call no more.

Still, Govind Singh didn't come.

As the sun dropped low and bats burst into flight from their daytime roosts, Dr. Sarma realized something: Govind Singh must no longer be in *musth*. He'd turned into a killer not because of his condition but because of the way the villagers had treated him. When the stressed elephant had tried to go home, he'd been shot at. The noise and commotion had likely triggered something in the already-frazzled elephant.

Dr. Sarma then realized something else: Govind Singh was different than any elephant he'd previously tried to subdue. And far more dangerous.

"We'll have to come back tomorrow and track him on foot," he told Narayan as the first stars appeared in the sky. "It's getting dark and it's not safe to pursue him tonight."

Narayan agreed, but as he opened the door to the truck, he hesitated. "Other captive elephants have been released into the forest since the logging ban," he said, referring to the 1996 decision by the Supreme Court of India to stop logging in government-owned forests. "We have to be sure we're targeting the correct bull. I know some local boys from the Singpho tribe. Govind Singh rampaged in the boys' village. They'll recognize him. Perhaps they could come and help us track him."

Dr. Sarma thought of the many dangerous situations he'd encountered over the years when tracking elephants. He didn't like the idea of bringing the boys on such a risky mission, but Narayan had a point. The boys would recognize the *makhna*. "Call them," he said. "We'll meet them here in the morning."

Narayan made the call, and then, exhausted, he and Dr. Sarma said goodbye to Kutum. They climbed into the truck and started off for the long drive back to the guesthouse.

They'd wake up early the next morning and return to try again.

～

That night after a dinner of *soal* fish curry, Dr. Sarma's favorite meal, they fell into a deep slumber. At five o'clock the next morning, as the birds broke out into their dawn chorus, the men climbed from their cots. Stiff from sleep but ready for the day, they drank their tea in silence and then set off again.

The two young Singpho boys were waiting for them when they arrived. With their wide smiles, the boys appeared excited for the adventure. Dr. Sarma greeted them, and the team of four headed off to look for Govind Singh.

As they stepped into the forest, a pair of endangered hoolock gibbons hooted. This was wild land, and though alert to dangers, Dr. Sarma felt at home. But that didn't make the terrain any easier. Thick mikania creepers and ferns made travel slow, and sometimes he could hardly see more than five feet ahead. Soon sweat dripped down his forehead, and still the vegetation grew denser.

Despite the difficult topography, Dr. Sarma kept his concentration. With each step, he listened for breaking branches and the loud gurgling stomach of an elephant. He searched the ground for tracks and trampled vegetation. He sniffed the air for the musky smell of elephant dung.

He caught a scent and was about to direct the group northward when he felt the wet tickle of blood on his wrist. He looked down and saw a leech attached to his skin. If there's one leech, there'll be more, he thought, recalling a previous trip tracking a rogue through a

forest much like this one. Balls of leeches had fallen
from the treetops, not to mention the thousands prowl-
ing the grass blades. He'd been so focused on his mission it wasn't until he arrived home and pulled off his
clothes for a bath that he'd realized he was covered with
the bloodsucking parasites.

"Everything OK?" Narayan asked, bringing Dr.
Sarma back to the present.

"Fine," he replied, peeling away the slimy creature
and dropping it. What could he do? Leeches and ants,
sweat and dirt, these discomforts were all parts of tracking and saving an elephant.

Another half hour passed, and still there was no sign
of Govind Singh. Now Dr. Sarma started to worry. It
was easier to spot an elephant in open land—safer, too.
In the thick forest an elephant had many places to hide,
which meant it was possible Govind Singh would see
them first.

It was far more dangerous to try to tranquilize an
elephant than to gun it down. A well-aimed shot at the
temple or the heart from a high-powered Magnum rifle
would stop an elephant in its tracks. Dr. Sarma's dart
only carried an immobilizing drug that would take 15
to 20 minutes to act—more than enough time for the
elephant to charge and kill the shooter. Narayan carried
a rifle, though Dr. Sarma knew his brother-in-law, with
his profound love of elephants, would have a hard time
using it.

He swatted a mosquito and wiped away sweat as he

thought about what to do. Should they turn around? Even if he did suggest going back, he knew Narayan would never agree to it. He also worried that when Govind Singh did eventually come out of the forest, the *makhna* would be certain to come into contact with humans. Dr. Sarma looked at his tired companions. He knew that if the elephant or any more villagers were killed, he'd feel responsible.

As if reading Dr. Sarma's mind, Narayan turned to his brother-in-law. "We can't quit now," he said. "Let's keep going."

Dr. Sarma nodded, and they continued. They'd just started walking again, though, when he stopped. He closed his eyes and noted the unmistakable smell of elephant dung. From the strong odor he knew it was fresh. Could this dung be from Govind Singh? He scanned the forest and listened for snapping branches.

Then, through an opening in the mikania creepers, he saw a huge *makhna* about 100 feet away. Dr. Sarma put a finger to his lips and pointed.

The younger of the two Singpho boys gasped. "It's him," he whispered. "Govind Singh."

Even as he recognized the danger, Dr. Sarma took in the animal's beauty—his massive head, spotted ears, and enormous size. The group was downwind of the elephant, so the animal—even with his incredible sense of smell, superior to that of any other land mammal—wouldn't detect them. But they were close, and they had to be careful.

Dr. Sarma quietly turned off the safety catch of the syringe projector. The rubber-soled shoes he'd worn today softened the impact of his steps. He gestured for the others to stay quiet. If anyone made even the slightest sound, Govind Singh, with his large ears acting as amplifiers, would discover the intruders—then who knew what could happen?

Dr. Sarma moistened his *gamosa,* a traditional Assamese hand-woven piece of cloth, and placed it over the mouth of the barrel to silence the sound. He raised the projector and straightened it on his shoulder. Just as he was about to shoot, the boy who'd identified the elephant took a step backward onto a twig.

The twig snapped a second before Dr. Sarma fired. The *makhna* turned in their direction just as the syringe discharged and hit him sideways in the rump. The angle was wrong—the dart didn't fully penetrate the animal's hide.

Dr. Sarma had time for just one word before Govind Singh charged: "Run!"

Without looking back, he raced away from the elephant, knowing that an enraged bull could outrun even the fastest sprinter for a short distance. He ran as fast as he could along a narrow cattle track. Govind Singh thundered through the forest, more like a racehorse than an elephant.

Dr. Sarma had no idea if anyone was with him or if he was alone. He could hear Govind Singh just feet behind him, though, and he knew he wouldn't escape by trying to outdistance the animal. His thighs and lungs burned. Branches scratched his face. Just as he thought Govind Singh would trample him, something flashed through his mind: elephants' poor vision—and the rumor that they can't make a quick turn. This was his only chance. He dove sideways into the thick undergrowth of a bamboo grove.

Deceived by Dr. Sarma's disappearance, Govind Singh kept charging straight ahead. Dr. Sarma didn't wait to see what would happen. He had to get away, and he had to find the others. He didn't even catch his breath before he started running again. He dodged branches and vines, sprinting to the west, down a hill, until he crossed some barbed wire that separated the forest from a tea estate.

The tea plants were a relief after the dense forest where he could hardly see anything, but he wasn't yet out of danger. A barbed wire fence was no challenge for the giant bull—and where were the others? But he couldn't run anymore. He collapsed to the ground, exhausted.

As he sat there, Dr. Sarma worried. What had happened to Narayan and the Singpho boys? Then he saw someone climbing over the fence. A second later the older of the two boys emerged from the forest. Dr. Sarma bolted up and ran to him.

The boy doubled over, trembling. "Govind Singh charged us. I ran away, but I got separated from the others."

Dr. Sarma didn't say another word. He started back toward the forest. He'd just gone a few steps when the younger boy climbed over the fence. He walked toward Dr. Sarma with his shoulders hunched, his head bowed.

Dr. Sarma took in the boy's body language and his throat tightened. "Where's Narayan?"

"He fell down . . . he couldn't get up . . . I shouted at him to shoot, but he refused." He paused and took a breath then in a hardly audible voice, said, "Govind Singh trampled him."

Dr. Sarma stared at the boy. Narayan dead? It couldn't be true, and yet it appeared it was. He knew how much his brother-in-law loved elephants, and now he'd given his life to save one. There was nothing he could do. He turned away from the others and sobbed.

On that November day in the Nalani Forest Reserve, Dr. Sarma's heart broke. Not only had he lost his dearest friend and brother-in-law, Narayan, a brave and committed conservationist, husband, and father, but he'd also failed to capture Govind Singh, who would later be killed by an official hunter hired by the government. Dr. Sarma's sister, Mani, had lost her husband, and her eight-year-old son had lost his father. Other people had lost loved ones, too, and there was one less elephant in an already-shrinking population.

These thoughts and the danger he was putting himself in weighed heavily on Dr. Sarma. He had children and a wife. Should he give up this aspect of his life and stop tracking elephants? If he stopped, who else was willing to do this work? Still he wondered, was it worth sacrificing his life?

∿

Two weeks after Narayan's death, Dr. Sarma got a call from a colleague, who explained that a bull elephant in Arunachal Pradesh was in *musth* and had escaped his *mahout*. The elephant had already killed one person. Would Dr. Sarma come and help?

The story was familiar, yet at the same time new. Each animal was an individual, each story important.

Just as he'd been forced to make a choice when he'd set out to track Manik, Dr. Sarma had to choose again now—only this time he understood the risks personally. His brother-in-law's death haunted him, but his love of elephants hadn't changed. Narayan had loved elephants, too, and Dr. Sarma felt certain that he wouldn't want him to give up. More than that, Dr. Sarma realized, he *couldn't* give up.

"I'll leave in an hour," he said.

COMMUNICATION
•
MY, WHAT BIG EARS YOU HAVE

"The beast which passeth all others in wit and mind."
—Aristotle

Bats "see" in the dark using echolocation: they send out high-pitched cries at frequencies above the range of human hearing and identify where objects are by listening to how the sound bounces back. Honeybee workers perform complex dances to teach other workers about the location of food sources hundreds of yards from the hive. Butterflies use ultraviolet markings to find a healthier mate. Other insects use the same ultraviolet rays to guide them to flowers.

These are just a few examples of the amazing range of communication types found in the animal world. There is endless variety to how various animals have adapted to perceive the world and communicate about it, and elephants are no exception.

An elephant's communication ranges from tactile to chemical, auditory to visual.

Tactile means perceived through touch—a fist bump or a hug, a high five or a back slap. Elephants touch each other a lot. They'll use their trunks, ears, tusks, feet, and tails to indicate everything from aggression to defensiveness to love to play. They may use their tusks to say, "Hey, good to see you," during a meeting. Or they may use them to lift a baby from the mud. Ears can be used to rub against one another affectionately, and tails to swat or to check the proximity of a calf.

They use their trunks the most, however, for tactile communication. This amazing appendage (a muscular, flexible extension of their upper lip and nose) is used to caress, explore, push, slap, reassure, and "shake hands." An elephant handshake? Actually, it's an elephant trunkshake. When one elephant greets another, it might insert the tip of its trunk into its companion's mouth. They might also twine their trunks together upon meeting. An elephant's trunk is both amazingly strong (with the help of the tusks, they can lift 600 pounds) and incredibly delicate (with the trunk's fingerlike extensions, an elephant can pluck a single blade of grass). It also has some of the most sensitive tissue ever studied. In fact, specialized cells in the trunk can pick up even the most subtle vibrations.

It isn't just their trunks that pick up vibrations, though. Their feet do too.

Sometimes elephants produce a deep, rumbling sound. When they do, the sound travels not only through the air, but also through the ground in what is called infrasound—sound too low to be heard by the human ear. If an elephant wants to talk to another elephant that is far away, it uses this low-frequency rumble. The sound waves move through the earth and can travel much farther than they do through the air—sometimes miles away! When an elephant senses a low rumble, it stops what it's doing and presses its heavily padded feet to the ground. The padding, filled with touch receptors, senses the vibration and sends a signal to the brain.

So, is this hearing or is it feeling? And does it even matter? It seems that in elephants these senses are blurred.

And since we're talking about rumbles, what about other elephant sounds?

We humans have an array of vocal communications. We sing. We laugh. We shout. We whisper. Elephants, too, have a vast assortment of acoustics. The trumpet is one of their most familiar sounds: Need an elephant sound in a film? Make it trumpet. Blasting air through the seven-foot trunk, an elephant basically has full-time access to a brass instrument!

But the trumpet certainly isn't their only sound. With a vocal range of about ten octaves (the best human singer in the world, by contrast, has a range of about three octaves) elephants have an extensive acoustic vocabulary. Within this range, they can make a lot of different sounds. They can bark, cry, grunt, snort, chirp (unique to Asian elephants), growl, and rumble. (The rumble, by the way, was given its name because it was once thought to emanate from the belly, like an upset stomach.) And just as you can recognize a friend or a family member by his or her unique voice, elephants can recognize each other by their sounds.

Perhaps even more amazing than an elephant's hearing is its sense of smell. Olfactory (scent) cues are key to elephant communication. If you have a dog, especially one in the hound group, you might have had the frustrating experience of taking your companion for a walk and having to stop every few feet to let it sniff. For a dog, even the smallest patch of ground holds an extravagant amount of information. If the world comes most alive for dogs through their noses, this is even more true for elephants. (Now imagine taking an elephant for a walk.)

The tip of an elephant's trunk is always on the move, sniffing out and learning about the elephant's environment. To put their sense of smell into perspective, elephants have a smelling surface area in their trunk equivalent to a living-room rug. Humans have the equivalent of a postage stamp. They also have a higher number of genes dedicated to smell than any other mammal—twice that of a dog and five times that of a human.

Elephants will often first touch the tip of their trunks to the ground (to detect pheromones in urine, like when a dog sniffs the pee of another dog on a tree) or to some part of another elephant (the temporal gland or genitals). They'll then bring their trunks to the roof of their mouths, where special sensory organs carry the chemical signal to the brain.

But what about visual communication? The world primarily comes to us eye-centered humans through images. We have what is called trichromatic vision, meaning we have three types of cone cells in our retina (the light-sensitive part of the eye): one type for sensing red light, another for blue, and one more for green. Elephants, however, only have two types of cone cells: one for sensing red and the other for green. This is called dichromatic vision. Forget the big words for a minute and focus on what this means practically. Having *di* (two) instead of *tri* (three) vision means that, in terms of color, elephants see the world about the same way a colorblind human does.

However, there is more to vision than color. Elephants spend about half their waking time in the light of day and half in the dark of night. Because of this, they've developed the ability to see in dim light as effectively as in full light. On a night with no moon, however, they're virtually blind.

These are just a few of the things humans know about how elephants communicate, but there's still much to learn about their mysterious and magical world. Maybe if we listen carefully enough, they'll tell us.

LOKHIMAI

•

2002

The years after Narayan's death were difficult. Dr. Sarma often felt sad and spent long periods thinking about his brother-in-law. He worked hard, burying his sorrow in his work, caring for his animal patients, tracking elephants, and saving more lives.

He'd found his calling and was living his dream, as his grandmother had predicted. But Dr. Sarma no longer felt like just an elephant doctor. He felt like a representative of the species.

His family mattered to him. His wife and children missed him when he was gone, and he missed them, too—yet most weekends were devoted to injured elephants. He couldn't stand to see one suffering. So when a man named Amir Hussein called one Saturday to tell

Dr. Sarma that his female elephant, Lokhimai, had a painful swelling on her back, Dr. Sarma listened, even though he'd sworn to take the day off.

"I hired her out for logging work in a private forest reserve in Arunachal Pradesh," Amir explained, referring to privately owned land where logging was still permitted. "She came back a week ago. The *mahout* used her to drag a few logs in another forest in a neighboring village after she returned. Yesterday we noticed the swelling."

"And what have you done to treat it?"

"Nothing," Amir admitted. "I don't know what to do. Can you help her?" He told Dr. Sarma that he lived in a small village called Dipila and asked if he could come.

Dr. Sarma suspected the elephant's swelling might be from an infection caused by an ill-fitting harness she wore when hauling logs. Treating an infection was easier than tracking a rogue, but he was in Guwahati, a two-hour drive from Dipila. It meant another day on the road, another day away from family.

Dr. Sarma weighed his plans to stay home against the sick and suffering animal's plight and decided to go. He'd hurry back as quickly as possible to be with his family.

"I'll be there in a few hours," he said.

Dr. Sarma assumed that caring for Lokhimai would be routine; he'd treat her as he had so many others and then move on. But his relationship with Lokhimai turned out to be anything but routine.

ᴨ

Dr. Sarma packed up his supplies and set off. On either side of the road, men in *lungis*—lengths of cloth wrapped around the body and tied at the waist—worked fields of cultivated rice. White birds soared in a cloudless sky. Eagles and hawks caught updrafts and rode these thermal winds. Village dogs, chickens, and cows lounged in the roads, creating an animal obstacle course that made progress slow.

Two hours after setting out, Dr. Sarma arrived at Amir's farm. With its corrugated tin roof and bamboo thatched walls, surrounded by sugarcane and rice, orange groves and mango trees, the house reminded him of his own childhood and his family's farm. He thought of Lakshmi and wondered what Lokhimai was like. Eager to meet her, he spoke briefly with Amir, then went to talk with Samsul, Lokhimai's *mahout,* in order to learn everything he could about the ailing elephant.

"She was always gentle and happy to see me," Samsul explained, squatting in the shade of a tree and chewing betel nut, which stained his teeth red. "But in the past few days she's been acting strangely. She keeps using the tip of her trunk to blow air or dust onto her back, and she moans and sways from side to side."

Dr. Sarma recognized the symptoms Samsul described. He started to wonder if Lokhimai might have a type of abscess, an inflamed area of the body containing pus, called a farra gall: one of the most common problems in captive elephants. Common, but serious—if the abscess wasn't cared for it could lead to severe complications. It could even lead to death.

Samsul brought Dr. Sarma to the orchard where Lokhimai stood tethered in a clearing of trees, her front legs hobbled to keep her from wandering off. She flapped her ears and squeaked when Dr. Sarma approached. He instantly felt tenderness toward her. The first thing he had to do, though, was observe her from a clinical point of view, not an emotional one, so that he could professionally assess her overall condition. In order to do this, he stood about ten feet away from the elephant and took in her appearance, recording in his notebook everything he saw.

On the first page he wrote:

Height: approximately eight feet

Weight: approximately three and a half tons

Skin around trunk, eyes, and the fold of her ears lightly freckled, still has most of its pigment.

He then used other clues, such as the outward folds at the upper borders of her ears (which fold more and more as an elephant gets older), to guess her age and noted that she was likely about thirty.

Next, he took in her small, heavily lashed, amber-colored eyes. Since she was a female, she didn't have tusks, but as she opened her mouth to reach for some leaves, Dr. Sarma saw the two small tusklike teeth called tushes.

He wanted to inspect the patient more closely, but before he approached, he spoke to Lokhimai in a soft, confident voice to gain her trust. "Hello," he said. "I'm sorry you're not well. I'm here to help. My name is KK."

As he'd learned to do the day Durgaprasad lashed out at Dr. Pathak, he observed Lokhimai's body language as he spoke. He watched her eyes and her posture, looking for any signs of aggression and letting the elephant tell him if she was ready for him to come closer. Of all the animals he'd treated in his practice, elephants were the most expressive, and through careful observation he knew he could learn much about both Lokhimai's mental state and physical condition.

As he studied her, Dr. Sarma saw that her eyes were soft and her body was relaxed, so he took a step forward and touched the left side of her face. He closed his eyes for a moment and ran his hand over the peaks and valleys of her wrinkled skin, letting the familiar stiff and bristly hairs poke his fingertips.

Lokhimai made a soft grunting sound and sniffed him with her trunk.

Dr. Sarma smiled and opened his eyes. "Nice to meet you, too," he said and stepped back so he could further observe her general body condition and attitude.

Although the sore back and what was likely an abscess were the obvious problems, he knew it was important to perform a thorough examination, as many conditions had multiple symptoms, some of which could be less apparent. Again, he got out his notebook and recorded what he saw.

Visible ribs, slightly emaciated, possibly from a season of strenuous logging and the 350-mile walk back home.

Lower back, which should be smooth and rounded in a healthy elephant, has a visible bony ridge.

The natural depression in her head is more concave in shape than in a healthy elephant.

"You're not feeling good, are you?" he murmured, touching her again—this time noting her skin's dry and somewhat scaly texture.

As if in response, Lokhimai reached up her trunk and touched Dr. Sarma's hand. An elephant's trunk is used for smelling, breathing, trumpeting, drinking, and with more than 40,000 muscles, it can just as easily pick up a heavy log as delicately hold a coin. Dr. Sarma also knew that the trunk could lash out and hurt a person, but this touch felt gentle and friendly: a greeting, as if she knew he'd come to help. Lokhimai then reached her trunk into Dr. Sarma's pocket.

"But you're still naughty," he teased, as she searched for a snack. He reached into his pocket and tossed a sweet apple into her eager mouth, which she opened wide, as if to receive a much larger jackfruit.

Dr. Sarma spoke to Lokhimai as he worked, and she communicated back, touching him with her trunk, making soft grunts and occasional moans that communicated her distress. He'd treated hundreds of elephants, but each one was unique. Lokhimai, he thought, seemed

like a particularly sensitive elephant. As the sun slanted
through the palm leaves and the smell of something
savory cooking on a fire reached his nose, he wished he
could spend the day enjoying her company. But he had
work to do.

He now looked more closely at Lokhimai's eyes. He
wanted to see if there were any abnormalities, such as
cataracts or scars. "I know," he said as she closed her
third eyelid—used, along with an elephant's long eye-
lashes, to keep out dust and debris. "You don't like having your eyes examined."

He stepped back, letting Lokhimai know he wouldn't
be touching her eyes, just observing. When she opened
them, he wrote what he noticed in his notes:

Eyes watery and a bit dull in color.

"Don't worry," he assured her, although he was actually quite worried, "I'm going to help you."

She replied with a soft chirping sound.

"Can you ask her to raise her trunk?" Dr. Sarma asked
Samsul.

"*Dalei,*" said the *mahout.*

Lokhimai raised her trunk as she'd been trained
to do at the command. Dr. Sarma leaned forward and
inspected her tushes to make sure there was no asymme-
try—unevenness between the two sides—which could
mean the nerves had been damaged. He also looked to
make sure there weren't any fissures or cracks in the

ivory, which could serve as an entry for infection into the nerve, causing the tushes to decay and the elephant to stop eating. Dr. Sarma then checked her tongue, careful not to put his hand in her mouth as an elephant can clamp down during an inspection and inflict serious injury. Finally, he looked at the rest of her teeth.

"Your teeth are looking good," he assured Lokhimai, who lowered her trunk and ripped off some leaves from a banana tree to eat.

Her teeth were in good condition, but her tongue, which should have been rosy and pink, was pale, another symptom that worried him. He wrote this down in his journal with his other notes.

"How about your feet?" he asked, continuing to talk to Lokhimai as he went through his checkup.

First he observed her legs for sign of swelling. Then he carefully rubbed his hands down each massive leg to see if she reacted and if any part felt tender. As he worked, Dr. Sarma listened for sounds of protest and watched her body language to see if his touch agitated her. Even though her front legs were hobbled, she could swat with her tail or hit with her trunk. Dr. Sarma knew she wouldn't hurt him on purpose, but she didn't know he was trying to help. Caring for an elephant was never completely safe. But the gentle elephant didn't protest. She made a few chirping sounds and flapped her ears as he worked.

Once he finished inspecting her legs, Dr. Sarma turned his attention to her feet. He had her raise each foot, one at a time, onto a stool and he looked at the digits. He then examined the number of toenails, usually five on the front and four on the back. However, since there can be variation, he made sure to count.

Again, he took out his notebook and wrote:

Three toenails on the back left foot

Overgrown cuticles

Dr. Sarma then threw some dust on her front foot to see if it would stick. It didn't, another sign that she wasn't well. The overgrown cuticles were blocking her sweat glands. He wrote down this observation.

Skin over the nails dry.

He listened to her heart and monitored her respiration, and then it was time to examine the wound. "Can you ask her to bend her knees?" he asked Samsul.

Samsul gave the *boith* command for Lokhimai to kneel, but she didn't obey. He gave the order again, and this time she rumbled in protest.

Dr. Sarma knew that it often hurt an elephant with a farra gall abscess to sit like that. If a farra gall was indeed the problem, he needed to think of another plan. If she couldn't lower herself to his height, he decided he'd rise to hers. "Can you bring me a ladder?"

Samsul nodded and went to retrieve the ladder, returning moments later and leaning it against a sturdy tree. He then guided Lokhimai to stand beside it. Dr. Sarma gripped the rungs and climbed up. When he reached the top, he peered into the treetops, where a ruby-cheeked sunbird flitted between red flowers. For a moment he felt like he was at the summit of the world. The feeling brought him back to his days with Lakshmi when he perched atop her lofty body and everything but his connection with the elephant faded away.

Lokhimai let out a low rumble, and Dr. Sarma turned his attention back to her. Now he had to check for infection. He closed his eyes and rubbed his hand along her spine, letting the texture and temperature beneath his fingers inform him of her condition. The area was hot and mildly swollen. Lokhimai pushed air through her trunk and groaned.

"You're in pain, aren't you?" he said in a soothing voice when he opened his eyes. "I understand. No more examination for now." He descended the ladder. When he stepped to the ground, Lokhimai reached out and touched him with her trunk. "Don't worry," he said again. "You'll get better soon."

But Dr. Sarma was worried. He picked up his notebook and found a plastic chair in the shade of a tree where he could sit and think. Clearly Lokhimai had an infection, and it had taken a toll on her health. As a goat bleated in the background and men in the fields called to one another, Dr. Sarma watched the elephant.

She hardly moved at all. Healthy elephants were never still. They were always swinging their trunks, flicking their tails, flapping their ears, dusting their backs with dirt, scratching their bodies with a broken twig held in their trunks. Lokhimai wasn't doing any of these things. Although she was eating, she was too still, too listless.

Dr. Sarma wrote all this down in his notes, then went to talk to Amir.

"What do you think?" Amir asked, visibly concerned.

Dr. Sarma took off his baseball cap and mopped his brow. "I think she has an abscess caused by an infection," he said. "I'll try to treat it with ice, astringent, and some local injections."

~~~

A flock of parrots feasted on the wild star fruits in Amir's garden as Dr. Sarma went to his truck for supplies. From a nearby mango tree, a cuckoo called in its sweet voice, *koo-oo-koo-oo*. Unlike the bird and its tranquil song, Dr. Sarma was tense. He had to get the infection under control. If he didn't, the abscess would spread under her skin, and Lokhimai could die.

The second he had his medicines and supplies prepared, Dr. Sarma returned to her. He climbed back up the ladder, placed an ice pack on her sore back, and waited to see how she'd react. Would she rumble and swat with her tail? Would she try to topple the ladder? Lokhimai just let out a few low rumbles.

"Good girl, my friend," he said, reassuring her with his soft, gentle voice.

After he cooled and numbed the wound, Dr. Sarma reached into his bag for a gel to help draw the tissue together and reduce the swelling. He hoped it would make Lokhimai more comfortable. He rubbed the gel into her thick skin and then climbed down from the ladder again to let her have a break.

As she tore at leaves with her trunk and sucked up water, Dr. Sarma turned to Samsul. "Now I have to give her a shot," he said, explaining about the steroid mixed with an antibiotic that he hoped would bring down the swelling and stop the infection.

Once again Dr. Sarma climbed up. First, he washed Lokhimai's back and her sides, as usual getting pricked by stiff hairs. Next, he scrubbed the area of dirt and dried it with a clean towel. Once the area was dry, he gently applied antiseptic. Finally, it was time for the shot.

As he fixed a syringe with the drug to a two-inch needle, his thoughts flashed to the time a cow elephant who didn't want her shot had kicked him and thrown him several yards. Except for his pride, he hadn't been hurt, but he hoped Lokhimai wouldn't react in a similar way.

"You're not going to like this, but it's for your own good," he told her.

And then he plunged the needle into her back.

Lokhimai flinched. Her powerful muscles tensed, but she didn't lash out. It was as if she trusted him and knew he was there to help.

"*Vakratunda mahakaya*—the curved-toothed, gigantic, noble animal," said Dr. Sarma, as he massaged the site of the injection and applied more antiseptic. "I'll be back to check on you."

∿

Dr. Sarma returned four days later as promised. The moment he saw Lokhimai, he saw that the swelling was still there. "I'll have to operate immediately to drain the abscess," he told Amir.

Amir agreed, and Dr. Sarma went to work. First, he gave Lokhimai a dose of strong sedative. Then he numbed the abscess area with local anesthetic. Finally, he made an incision over the wound.

As soon as the incision was made, more than half a gallon of pus erupted. The fluid didn't faze Dr. Sarma. This was all part of his job. He kept working, next removing a large area of skin and damaged tissue. The removal of the skin would cause a big scar, but Dr. Sarma could at last relax. He felt certain that Lokhimai would be OK.

"Goodbye for now," he said. "I'll be back to see how you're doing."

∿

Every other day for a month, Dr. Sarma returned to clean Lokhimai's wound and to change her bandage, driving to Dipila after work and on weekends. Each time he came, he brought the elephant a treat. Sometimes be brought her sweet bread, other times a jackfruit, some pieces of sugarcane, an apple, a banana, or even some sweet pineapple. He always spoke to her, whispering words in Assamese.

Dr. Sarma often sat with Lokhimai until late in the quiet evening. It wasn't until the moon rose and the village grew dark that he'd say goodbye and drive back home. He'd loved Lakshmi, his first elephant, and now it was like falling in love again. He pined for Lokhimai when they weren't together and rejoiced when they were.

As the weeks passed, Lokhimai started flapping her ears, swinging her trunk, flicking her tail, and dusting her back with dirt. Dr. Sarma was happy to see his elephant companion feeling better.

After a month, it was time to say goodbye. Lokhimai no longer required his care. "Be well, my friend," he said on his last visit, as he stroked her trunk and gave her one more banana.

Dr. Sarma was thrilled to see her feeling better and relieved to know she'd be OK, yet he was also sad. It was likely he'd never see her again. With this thought on his mind, he cried silently as he drove away.

Little did he know that one day in the future something extraordinary would happen.

WHAT DOES TEA HAVE TO DO WITH ELEPHANTS?

"Elephants are hungry. Their stomachs are empty. They are like tsunamis and will break through your houses and raid crops. But if you create a refuge, they will visit your villages, but they will visit like gentle ocean waves."
—KK Sarma

Imagine a hot July day. No school. No homework. The smell of freshly cut grass tickles your nose. The earth is cool under your bare legs as you sit in the shade of an old tree, listening to music, sipping a glass of cold iced tea.

In Assam, things are a little different. The temperature reaches 100 degrees Fahrenheit (37.8 degrees Celsius). The sky is dark, heavy with thick clouds. No weather forecast is needed to know it will rain. Summer in northeastern India means monsoons: 10 to 12 inches

(25 to 30 centimeters) of rain a day pelt down on this landscape of vast tea plantations, paddy fields, and isolated patches of forest.

In the fields of one of the tea plantations, a fifteen-year-old Adivasi girl kneels and plucks a handful of shiny, green leaves. The leaves she picks will be processed and exported all over the world for high-quality black tea, perhaps ending up in the glass you're now drinking. As the girl works, she hears breaking branches, squeaking, trumpeting, and low rumbling. The sounds can only mean one thing: elephants.

She looks up and sees a herd of cows and calves plodding along the edge of the field, trunks sniffing the air, babies bunched up close to their mothers. The oldest elephant leads the group in search of food, water, and shade. For decades she's been in charge of this annual journey, migrating from the hills of Bhutan to the valley of the Brahmaputra River in Assam. For thousands of years, her ancestors have followed the same route.

But now, as the dark sky crackles with the promise of monsoon rain, there's nothing for the herd to eat. They try to drink, but the water tastes funny, tainted with pesticides. By the end of the day they're hungry, thirsty, and tired. They must move on. They must find a way to survive. But how? And more importantly, where?

∿

In 1800 jungles, grasslands, and wetlands covered Assam. Elephants, Royal Bengal tigers, clouded leopards, one-

Elephants spend their day in tea plantations where there is shelter but nothing they can eat or drink.

horned rhinos, swamp deer, and wild buffalo roamed the valleys, forests, and hills. Huge adjutant storks, many species of vultures, chestnut-headed bee-eaters, Asian fairy-bluebirds, wreathed hornbills, purple sunbirds, and crested serpent eagles filled the skies.

Now, jump ahead twenty-three years. Some might tell the story like this: Robert Bruce, a Scottish explorer, finds Assam tea growing in the wild while in the region for trading purposes. He meets an Assamese nobleman named Maniram Dutta Baruah, popularly known as Maniram Dewan, who takes Bruce to meet Bessa Gam, the local Singpho chief. Bessa Gam cordially provides

Bruce with samples of tea leaves and seeds, which Bruce sends to England. Hence, the discovery of Assam tea belongs to an adventurous Scottish chap.

The Singpho might tell the story like this: they'd been drinking tea and using the leaves in their food for seven centuries before Bruce's arrival. They'd eaten tea leaves as a vegetable prepared in mustard oil and garlic. One ancient recipe called *letpet* used fermented leaves, mixed with oil, garlic, fried shrimp, fruit, and coconut. Hence, the discovery of Assam tea belonged to the Singpho.

Perhaps, then, it's correct to say that the Singpho discovered the tea while Bruce brought it to the Western world. Regardless of how this black tea was "discovered," nothing in Assam has been the same since.

∿

If you look at a map of North America before the arrival of Europeans, you'll see that half of the whole continent was forest. Imagine the great packs of wolves, the massive grizzly bears, the flocks of passenger pigeons so vast they darkened the skies for days that used to thrive there. Then settlers cleared the lands, mostly for agriculture. And with the clearing of habitat (or in the case of the pigeons, hunting), species went extinct or else were driven into the small fragments of remaining forest.

The same thing happened in Assam. Soon after Bruce introduced the tea to the Western world, the East India Company wanted to start selling it. This huge English trading company ruled large areas of India, including Assam, until the British crown took over. And in the eyes of the company, forests might as well be wasteland. Who wanted useless jungle when tea was making money? People were in a hurry to profit off this new crop.

Rid the soil of the jungle! the East India Company said.

Free land if you clear 10 percent each year! they advertised.

Fell the trees! they ordered.

And people did. The first tea estate was established in 1837. The first eight chests of leaves were shipped to London in 1838. And by the end of the 19th century, Assam became the second-largest tea-producing region in the world. (China is the first.) Today the tea estates of Assam grow millions of pounds of tea a year. All this means that not a lot of food, water, shelter, or space is left.

And here's the thing about elephants: they need a lot of these things. Specifically, they require 300 to 500 pounds of food each day, 70 gallons of water per day, and about 100 to 200 square miles of territory to roam. Wouldn't you need this much food, water, and space if you weighed more than 6,000 pounds?

So you see the problem. With 10 percent of the world's remaining Asian elephants living in Assam—about 5,000 wild ones—and thousands of large and small tea plantations dominating the land, survival for these huge herbivores is tricky. In most plantations, there's not a blade of grass for elephants to eat, not a drop of clean water for them to drink.

Tea plantations could be their demise.

But they could also be their hope.

Some tea farmers are working to create habitat on their land for elephants. Their tea is certified as elephant friendly, meaning they leave a small refuge for elephants. No tea is grown in this patch of land. No pesticides are used. No trees are cut. No fences block the elephants' movement. This habitat might not be large enough for a herd to depend on solely, but if enough farmers leave bamboo, fruit trees, and elephant grass—all foods the elephants love—the patches will be connected like a trail, and elephants might be able to survive.

Elephant-friendly tea is good for elephants. It's good for farmers, too, because a nonprofit group (which you can learn about in the afterword) sells this tea and gives a percentage of every sale back to them to protect more elephants. It's good for local people because when elephants have habitat, they don't wander into villages in search of food. And best of all, it tastes good, which means it's good for tea drinkers, too.

THE WILD BULL OF PANERI TEA ESTATE
•
2012

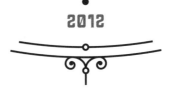

Dr. Sarma often wondered how Lokhimai was doing. He missed seeing his friend, but he had so many responsibilities that over time he lost track of her. This didn't mean the elephant wasn't in his heart—he was just very busy. He was promoted to head of the Department of Surgery and Radiology in the College of Veterinary Science. His children were growing up. His daughter wanted to follow in his footsteps and become a veterinarian, while his son became a bodybuilder and fell in love with motorbikes.

There were changes in the land, too. Many more forests in Assam were converted into tea plantations, while at the same time tens of thousands of people poured into

Dr. Sarma works to save an elephant that was hit by a train.

the region from neighboring countries. These changes were hard on elephants.

Dr. Sarma did everything he could in his role as a veterinarian to protect the species. He met with government officials and company executives to discuss solutions for train tracks and power lines that often killed elephants. He worked with rural people to educate them about coexistence with elephants. He gave talks and lectures and taught his students about elephant care.

Sometimes, though, protecting the species meant saving one of its individual members.

ᴨᴫᴨ

On a Monday in May 2012, a forest department warden called Dr. Sarma to say that a young, wild tusker had been injured at the Paneri Tea Estate, several hours from Guwahati.

Dr. Sarma closed his eyes and thought about all the times he'd been called to help an elephant that had been injured in a tea plantation. Calves fell into ditches and couldn't get out. Adults ate pesticides or herbicides that had been sprayed on the crops or that hadn't been adequately stored.

"He touched a sagging power line," the warden explained. "He's been electrocuted."

Dr. Sarma sighed. An elephant's sensitive and soft padded feet conduct electric current, and more often than not, coming into contact with an electric fence means death for an elephant. Sometimes farmers intentionally let lethal power lines sag to deter crop-raiding elephants. Other times the drooping lines weren't intentional, and people complained to the electric companies, asking to have the dangerous power lines fixed, but the companies didn't respond. Either way, the results were the same.

"Is he still alive?" Dr. Sarma asked, fearing he was being called to conduct a postmortem examination of the bull.

"He's still alive, but he's lying on the ground, and he can't get up," the warden said. "The local vet is certain he'll die. That's why I called you. Do you think you can help?"

"I'll come," said Dr. Sarma, glancing at the clock, "but it will be three or four hours before I can get there. Let me talk to the vet who's with him."

When Dr. Anil Bora, the local veterinarian, came on the line, Dr. Sarma asked for more information about the animal's condition. Knowing that the young vet—who'd previously been his student—didn't have much experience with elephants, Dr. Sarma gave instructions. "You need to give the elephant steroids, antihistamines, and intravenous fluids," he said. "You also need to spray water on his body to keep him cool so he doesn't suffer from hyperthermia in the hot sun."

Dr. Bora said he'd try, but Dr. Sarma was worried. He'd have to get there as quickly as possible. As soon as he hung up, he rushed to collect the medicines he'd need. Once he had his supplies, he found someone to teach his morning classes. He wouldn't make it to the university today.

This was an emergency.

Despite his urgency, progress was slow. The traffic on the bridge over the Brahmaputra River was backed up for miles. Lines of trucks, motorcycles, bicycles, and rickshaws clogged the road. It felt as if all of India, with its population of over one billion people, had gathered in this one location.

Finally, the traffic started to move, and Dr. Sarma raced onward. When he reached the tea estate two hours later, though, he again had to slow down. Thousands of Adivasi tea pickers, Bodo tribal people, ethnic Assamese, and Nepalese who lived in the area had gathered by a flimsy barbed wire fence that separated the tea plantation where the elephant lay from the road.

Huge crowds of people always came to watch when an elephant was hurt. Although many people were afraid of elephants and disliked them when one ate their crops, Hindus also revered elephants, an animal they saw as the living embodiment of Lord Ganesha.

Right now, Dr. Sarma only cared about getting to the injured bull. He honked and shouted out his window. "Please move out of the way!" he called into the commotion. He honked and shouted, honked and shouted, until people cleared a path. Again he was able to slowly advance.

Finally, he made it to the elephant. He got out of his car and looked at the bull, lying on his side in a pit of mud.

"I poured water on him as you suggested," said Dr. Bora.

Dr. Sarma nodded, realizing his instructions to cool the elephant with water had been taken a bit too seriously. He'd meant for Dr. Bora to sprinkle water, not dump entire truckloads of it. He didn't want to criticize the vet's good intention, though, so he thanked him and tried to figure out how to navigate the mud that would surely be past his ankles.

But the mud was just part of the problem. The other problem was that the anguished tusker was kicking and thrashing. Getting close to him would be impossible.

"He's been circling and kicking like this for hours," Dr. Bora said. "I couldn't approach him to give the medicines and intravenous fluids you requested."

Dr. Sarma took in this troubling news as he paced the perimeter of the mud, stroking his mustache and thinking. If he were going to save the bull, he'd have to act quickly. The electrocuted elephant couldn't survive in this state much longer.

That's when he noticed something else. It wasn't just a human crowd who'd gathered to watch. About 500 yards away, a herd of elephants, old and young, peered out from the trees at the edge of the plantation. *It must be the young tusker's herd,* he thought. *They must be waiting for him to come back.*

The wounded bull rumbled. Was he talking to his family? Dr. Sarma knew that elephants had complex and varied vocalizations. Some sounds were transmitted through the ground and too low to hear. What was the animal saying? Was he asking for help?

"You can't give up. Your family is waiting for you," Dr. Sarma told the injured elephant. "You need to join them."

He looked desperately around the tea plantation for inspiration. He searched the rows of plants, the rusty bicycles leaning against the fence, the sheds and huts where materials were stored. One of the huts had been destroyed. Dr. Sarma gazed at the smashed bamboo walls, the shredded burlap bags, crumpled corrugated tin roof, and flattened plastic chair. Elephants often raided and destroyed fragile village homes and other buildings, not because they were malicious but because they were hungry. He figured that's what had happened here.

Dr. Sarma felt sad as he stared at the demolished hut, but the piles of building materials also gave him an idea. He spun around to Dr. Bora. "Can you go to that hut and get me four strong wooden poles?"

The young vet didn't ask why. He and two other men hurried off, returning several minutes later with the poles balanced across their shoulders. Dr. Sarma tucked one of the sturdy poles under his arm and stepped into cold mud that instantly seeped through his pants. His boots sloshed, sticking in the sludge that threatened to steal them off his feet. He had to be careful not just of losing a boot and slipping, but also of a possible head butt. One strong hit from the tusker's massive head could kill him, or at least break his legs.

Dr. Sarma felt the eyes of the humans and elephants watching him, but he blocked out all distraction. The pole was heavy and threatened to throw him off balance. He had to focus and plan each step so that he didn't lose his footing.

As he got close to the bull, the elephant trumpeted. "Easy," Dr. Sarma murmured, knowing how scared he must be. He pulled the pole from under his arm and planted it vertically in the mud next to the elephant's head. "Quickly now," he called to Dr. Bora. "Hand me another!"

Dr. Bora passed Dr. Sarma the next pole. He placed

this one on the other side of the bull's head. He took the next two poles and repeated the process, this time planting them on the sides of the animal's body. He had no idea if the poles would keep the elephant from thrashing, but before he could think much about it the tusker bellowed and tried to move.

"It worked!" Dr. Sarma exclaimed when the poles kept the animal in position. He turned again to Dr. Bora. "Hand me the medicine you prepared. Fast, we don't have much time." He had no idea how long the poles would keep him still.

Dr. Sarma took the needle, then reached out his mud-spattered hand and grabbed the elephant's freckled ear. He quickly located a vein and injected the medicines he hoped would help with the kidney damage and abnormal acid in his blood caused by the electrocution. "Your family's close by. You have to fight," he kept telling the bull while he administered bottle after bottle of the intravenous glucose.

His back and shoulders ached. He had no idea how much time had passed. Was it a minute or an hour? Finally, he gave the animal the last injection. Then he pulled the poles from the mud and stepped backward onto dry ground. There was nothing more he could do.

"Now what?" asked Dr. Bora.

"We wait for him to get up."

But the tusker didn't move.

The elephant, though out of immediate danger, was dehydrated and exhausted from his ordeal. Dr. Sarma was also exhausted from *his* ordeal. He was thirsty and hungry, covered with mud and sweat, but he didn't care. He needed another plan. If the elephant didn't get up, he would certainly die.

He glanced from the crowd of human onlookers to the wild elephant herd. As he looked at the elephants, he thought about his own children and the love he felt for them. He believed his love was the same love the elephants felt for their families. He couldn't let the elephants down.

That's when he noticed the forklift parked along the far fence line.

Dr. Sarma rushed over to the young man standing next to the machine. "Can you drive the forklift to help lift the elephant?"

The man stared at Dr. Sarma. "I can," he said with hesitation. "But what if he attacks us? A bull elephant can easily destroy a truck—and the people inside it."

Dr. Sarma knew that what the man said was true. He'd seen the result of just such a thing, a mangled truck and the people who'd been killed. But now wasn't the time to hesitate. He had to get the elephant to his feet. He wouldn't speculate on what would happen after that. "You only die once," he said and climbed into the passenger seat.

The man sighed and climbed in next to him.

"Insert the forks into the ground several feet away from him, so he doesn't get hurt," Dr. Sarma instructed, as the man turned the keys in the ignition.

The man nodded and maneuvered the machine's forklift into the mud several feet away from the tusker. But the whir of the engine scared the elephant. He trumpeted, kicked the ground, and changed position.

"Try again. This time move in very slowly," Dr. Sarma said, leaning forward in his seat.

Again, the man drove the forklift toward the elephant. Dr. Sarma felt his breath catch as he watched the young man finesse the forks beneath the elephant's massive body. Slowly, the machine elevated the animal to a sitting position.

"Reverse, now quickly!" Dr. Sarma exclaimed.

They were just feet away from the bull. If he stood and charged, he'd no doubt trample them. Or maybe he wouldn't get up at all. Maybe he was too weak, and the electrocution had done too much damage for him to recover.

"Come on," he whispered, urging the tusker to stand.

The elephant paused for another moment, then tried to rise. The mud was too slippery. He fell. The tusker tried again. This time he gathered all his strength, and with a determined burst of muscle and energy, he rose. The elephant's muscles trembled as he tested his feet. But he took one tentative step, then another.

"*Come on,*" Dr. Sarma whispered.

The animal slowly climbed out of the mud. He took a careful step away from the forklift and made it onto the dry grass.

For a moment the elephant just stood there, not

seeming to care about the mud covering his hide. Then he turned and looked directly into Dr. Sarma's eyes. Neither man nor elephant blinked. Neither man nor elephant moved. Dr. Sarma felt his eyes fill with tears. It was as if the bull was thanking him.

Suddenly, from across the tea estate, one of the wild elephants trumpeted. The call broke the young elephant's gaze. He looked away, lifted his trunk, and called back. After throwing a final glance at Dr. Sarma, the tusker went to join his family.

MATRIARCHS AND MEMORY
•
LISTEN TO YOUR ELDERS

"No individual or individual personality has more impact on family structure and fortunes than the matriarch, or female leader, of an elephant family."
—ElephantVoices

Just like you, an elephant has a family. Unlike a human, though, who can have a variety of family structures from tight-knit and small to large and extended, an elephant's family consists of an older female, her sisters, their adult daughters, and all their female children. Juvenile males leave the family and wander on their own, though they may group with older mentor males.

There is one elephant who's in charge of this tight-knit group: the matriarch, usually the oldest and largest female of the herd.

Perhaps you have a grandmother who likes to tell stories and show pictures of distant relatives and faraway places. She brings out the photo album and together you flip through the pages. Or maybe she shares a family tradition, a recipe, or a song, or tells you of the places she used to go as a girl. Like a grandmother, an elephant matriarch is the living historian of the herd. The past is etched into her mind, especially the land, the places where once she found food and water.

A herd's survival depends on her memory.

If there's a drought, for example, an experienced matriarch can lead her family to a source of water only she remembers. And in parts of Assam, elephants move between the hills of Bhutan and the flatlands of the Brahmaputra valley. The matriarch leads them on this long biannual journey. Without her memory, their ancient migratory path would be forgotten.

Just as all humans aren't the same, not all elephants—and therefore not all matriarchs—are the same. A matriarch might be calm, or she might be anxious. She might be indecisive, or she might be bold. Regardless of her disposition, a matriarch's personality sets the tone of the tribe. Maybe she's highly social and has a dear old friend in another herd. Away they go! The family heads out for a visit to this bond group (another herd with whom they're friendly). Each herd is part of a widening social network. The largest grouping of herds is called a clan, which can be composed of hundreds of elephants. It's similar to how you are part of a specific class at school, but all the different classes connect to form a wider community.

One thing all matriarchs have in common is respect. Think for a moment about the kind of leader you feel comfortable following. How do the parents, teachers, and mentors in your life earn your respect? And if you're a leader (president of a club, for example), how do you earn respect from others? For a matriarch elephant, respect is earned through wisdom, compassion, confidence, and connection.

A matriarch isn't a self-appointed bully. She doesn't fight her way to the top. She doesn't need to show off in order to get others to listen. The herd follows her because she's earned their trust. She's made good decisions. She has social knowledge of the individuals in her family and ecological knowledge of the land. She's shown bravery and confidence in a crisis, such as when facing a predator. She's demonstrated skill in navigating conflict. She's built and maintained close bonds within her family and in larger bond groups with other families. She's led by bringing the herd together, not by division or dominance.

She's also a teacher. Again, like a grandmother who helps her own daughter with the new and sometimes overwhelming responsibilities of taking care of a baby, a matriarch teaches the younger mothers how to care for their calves. An elephant might not have to change diapers, but she does have to learn how to nurse her young, how to help her calf to its feet when it stumbles. She has

An older female with a young elephant.

to teach a calf everything about being an elephant, even, believe it or not, how to use its trunk. When it's little, a calf swings around its trunk as if to say, "What's this thing for?"

Ideally, by the time a matriarch dies of natural causes, one of her older daughters will have gained the wisdom, experience, and memory needed to take over. But if a matriarch is killed, perhaps by a poacher—a very real threat for both African and Asian elephants—then the whole herd suffers. They lose their leader, their teacher, and their grandmother. They absorb the trauma and likely become more aggressive toward humans. And to make matters worse, the family might split up. The matriarch and her memories are key to a herd's strength. They are also key to its survival.

Above all, a matriarch cares for her family. The babies play under her watchful eyes. She and the other elders cherish the young. She keeps the extended family together. Elephants are joyful. They're playful, and they love their family.

Perhaps we're not as different from them as our appearance might suggest.

manimala, alaka, and shankar

•

2015

Using the poles and forklift to save the electrocuted tusker taught Dr. Sarma a great deal about improvising in the field where there are no guides or manuals for how to help and, in many cases, to save an elephant.

After the Paneri Tea Estate rescue, he had many chances to test his creativity. Once, when deep in the forests of Arunachal Pradesh, Dr. Sarma enlisted two *koonkies* to lift an injured wild elephant that had been shot and couldn't get up. By tying a heavy branch to the injured elephant and then using ropes to attach the branch to the *koonkies,* the two work elephants raised their wild brother to his feet. Another time, he used two abandoned truck tires as a pillow to help an old bull raise his head and make an opening for passage of soft ropes to help lift the elephant.

The wild elephants he rescued returned to their herds, and Dr. Sarma never saw them again. As for the captive ones he treated, sometimes they were traded or sold and left Assam to live in other parts of the country. He seldom saw these elephants again either. Still, he missed all those he'd cared for. He often thought about his patients and wondered what had become of them, especially those like Lokhimai, whom he had spent a long time with. What had happened to her? Was she thriving? Would she remember him if they saw each other again?

Some elephants certainly did remember him, but not in the loving way Dr. Sarma longed for. These elephants were the *koonkies* at forest department camps across the state. Three times a year, Dr. Sarma ran free health-care clinics to treat these work elephants. Often his treatment required giving the elephants shots, poking and prodding to assess their health. They remembered the doctor and his needles and grumbled. Sometimes they even tried to sneak away when they saw him coming!

In 2015, during the Muslim festival of Eid, celebrated after a month of daily fasting during Ramadan, Dr. Sarma was running a weekend of these free elephant health-care clinics. He left home early in the morning and drove to his first stop at a forest department camp in Orang National Park. One-horned rhinos, pygmy hogs, leopards, Royal Bengal tigers, and elephants lived there together in the wild.

Dr. Sarma improvising in the field to help an injured wild elephant.

As he approached the park, Dr. Sarma stopped by a swampy meadow to watch a group of one-horned rhinos with cattle egrets perched on their backs probing for ticks. He didn't linger for long, though. He was eager to see the elephants—even if those he'd given shots to three months earlier wouldn't be eager to see him.

At 9:00 AM the trumpeting of elephants greeted Dr. Sarma as he arrived in the park. He smiled and shook hands with each *mahout* and forest department warden and then drank a much-appreciated cup of tea. Once he finished his tea and spoke to the head warden about the morning's plan, Dr. Sarma set up his vaccinations on an old wooden table and perched on a plastic chair in the shade.

One by one, six *mahouts* brought the elephants to Dr. Sarma—three *makhnas*, one tusker, and two females. The elephants waited their turn for treatment under a leafy canopy, touching each other with their trunks, trumpeting and chirping at their friends. For the elephants, it was social time. For Dr. Sarma, it was work.

"I'm ready for my first patient," he told a young *mahout* when he finished setting up his medicines and equipment.

The *mahout* led Manimala, an old cow with speckled ears and a slow gait, to him. Dr. Sarma had given Manimala a shot at her checkup three months earlier. On this day, all she and the other elephants needed were vaccinations against worms and parasites, but he knew she'd remember being poked with his needle. As he mixed Manimala's vaccines with boiled sugarcane and rice, he wondered how she'd react.

When he finished mixing the medicine, he put it in a metal bowl and placed the bowl on the ground. Manimala stood in front of the table, towering over him, her front legs hobbled, her *mahout* at her side. But she didn't eat.

She just looked at Dr. Sarma and grumbled, as if to say, "I know you put medicine in there. I can smell it. You can't trick me."

Dr. Sarma understood that Manimala, like all elephants, wasn't just clever, she was also a master chemist, analyzing the world through scent. "It's for your own good," he scolded, as if she were a child who could be reasoned with.

Manimala flapped her ears. She blinked away a fly.

"Eat, or you'll get sick," Dr. Sarma continued, still trying to convince the elephant of his human logic.

Finally, Manimala reached into the bowl. Using the appendage at the tip of her trunk known as a finger, she brought a small bite of food to her mouth. Dr. Sarma stiffened in his seat and waited to see what would happen.

Manimala was the matriarch at this camp. The other elephants were watching. They'd follow her direction. If she didn't eat, neither would they.

Manimala grumbled again, but she took another bite of food. Dr. Sarma exhaled and sank back into the chair. The other elephants would now also eat their food and get their vaccinations.

Elephant by elephant, Dr. Sarma checked them all. He touched and poked, prodded and assessed each one's health. As he worked, he wondered if the elephants knew that for him this was more than just a job? The little boy who'd first fallen in love with Lakshmi lived inside him, but did the elephants know that? Could they feel the love in his hands? He wasn't sure, but none of them swatted or slapped or tried to sneak away. For this, Dr. Sarma was grateful.

As the day grew hot, the birdsong died down and a pair of hornbills glided overhead. Finally, he finished his examinations. He said goodbye to the elephants, goodbye to the *mahouts* and the forest wardens, then packed his supplies to leave.

"I'll see you in three months," he told the head warden. "Of course, call me if you need anything before then."

He got into his car and, with a final glance over his shoulder, drove off to Satsimalu camp thirty miles away. He sang as the car rattled down the road, happily crooning his favorite Hindi tunes. At Satsimalu camp he'd be looking after another old cow, Alaka, as well as her four-year-old twins and her new baby. This was a special visit. There were only three pairs of Asian elephant twins in the world. Plus, how could he resist the sweetness of a calf?

As he drove, Dr. Sarma recalled the last calf he'd helped, a wild female he'd rescued a few years earlier. The calf had fallen into a ditch in a tea plantation, but pulling her out had been the easy part. Reuniting her with her mother had been much harder. Elephant calves quickly bond with humans and often a herd won't take them back.

The car bumped up the dirt road toward Satsimalu camp and he thought about what had happened that day. Once he'd pulled the calf from the ditch and had her stabilized, he'd offered her a bottle with milky baby formula. The second she reached for it, though, he'd pulled his hand back, letting her cry out. He'd repeated this cruel trick several times, hoping her mother would hear the cries of her baby and come for her.

Dr. Sarma prepares medicine for a captive elephant at one of his free health-care camps.

It worked! The mother came thundering from the trees. But then she retreated. He remembered the devastating squeaks and cries of the calf, how he'd felt his own heart breaking on the baby's behalf. He'd been certain she'd be orphaned and face a life in captivity. But then the mother returned. She'd sprayed a trunk full of water all over her baby before allowing the startled calf to suckle. And then he'd understood. A good bath was all the calf needed. Her mother had washed away the human smell. She'd made her an elephant again.

But now he was at the camp and his thoughts returned to Alaka. He parked in front of the forest department headquarters, a cinderblock building with peeling blue paint and a rusted tin roof, and got out of the car. Mr. Rai, the camp's head warden, came out to greet him.

Before Dr. Sarma could even answer Mr. Rai's question about his health, the curious elephant twins, who were lingering in the grass in front of the building near their mother, approached to investigate his pockets. They shoved at his legs, knocked into his knees, and acted like the young, unruly children they were. The twins were bolder than they'd been at his last visit. Taller too, he noted, smiling down at the mischievous youngsters. Their curved backs now cleared his waist. He patted each one and offered them some sugarcane.

"You're looking good," he told them. "No need for an examination today."

The twins soon got bored. They turned their attention to something new that caught their eyes, a bird on a branch or some tasty leaves. Dr. Sarma focused on Alaka.

The old cow stood in the shade, her newborn baby tucked carefully beneath her massive torso. Alaka knew Dr. Sarma, but her focus wasn't on him. All of her attention was on her calf. She fondled the baby with her trunk, speaking to her in the intimate language between a mother elephant and her young.

As Dr. Sarma watched the pair, he thought about what amazing mothers elephants were. Their pregnancy lasted for 19 to 21 months, and the offspring would often stay with their mothers for the rest of their lives.

He also worried. Alaka was now 66. She'd already given birth to seven calves, mostly from mating with wild bulls. What would happen to her if another wild bull were to come around? She wouldn't survive another pregnancy. Though she was a captive elephant, she lived without an enclosure and foraged in the wild. Her hobbled front legs kept her from wandering off.

The baby made a low, soft groan, and Dr. Sarma looked at her more closely.

What he saw startled him. She lay on her side in the dirt, not even reacting to the flies and mosquitoes buzzing around her ears and eyes. Worse, her wrinkled skin bagged around her bones like a loose-fitting dress. She was much too thin. Dr. Sarma knew that a protective mother elephant would never let him approach her baby for an examination, but he didn't need to get closer. It was obvious that the calf wasn't well.

He turned to Mr. Rai. "The baby's too skinny. Isn't she eating?"

Mr. Rai shook his head and sighed. "Alaka isn't producing enough, and what milk she makes, the twins take."

"The twins are too old to be nursing!" Dr. Sarma exclaimed. "They have to be weaned immediately. The baby won't survive without milk."

He had to do something right away. The cow was old, and her milk supply was low even without the greedy twins taking it all. He sped to his car and mixed some mineral supplements with soft cooked banana stems. At her advanced age, Alaka had already worn down her teeth and could no longer grind her own food. The soft banana would allow her to take the supplements. He'd do his best to help her produce more milk, but even with the supplements, he worried she wouldn't make enough.

He returned to Alaka and approached her slowly from her left side, talking to her as he advanced. He saw in her eyes that she was tired. "I brought this for you," he murmured and put the food on the ground in front of her.

Alaka stood still and silent, but she accepted the soft nourishment he provided. Dr. Sarma watched as she ate, one small bite at a time. She had a quiet dignity about her, the wisdom of an elder. *And the baby, so fragile,* he thought. At this young age, she didn't even know how to use her trunk.

What else could he do to help?

Then he got an idea. He turned to Mr. Rai. "You'll have to buy baby formula for the infant if Alaka's own supply doesn't get better."

"But we can't afford that!" Mr. Rai protested.

Dr. Sarma knew it was a huge challenge for the forest department with its small budget to purchase formula for the baby. Mr. Rai's anxious expression confirmed this fact. "Don't worry," he said, accepting that he'd pay for this out of his pocket. "As soon as I finish at the other camps, I'll drive to the nearest town, buy some formula, and return."

Mr. Rai gratefully accepted the offer, and Dr. Sarma checked his watch. He had to get going. He had more elephants to tend to. He said goodbye to the elephants, goodbye to Mr. Rai, and went to his car.

He was just packing up his equipment when the phone rang.

"My name is Mr. Choudhury," the caller said. "I heard you're the elephant doctor. I'm calling because my *makhna*, Shankar, is very sick."

"What's wrong with him?" asked Dr. Sarma.

"Our family shares ownership of Shankar with another family who lives about 200 miles away from us," Mr. Choudhury explained. "He used to be a logging elephant. The family asked to see Shankar, so our *mahout*, Rahman, took him to them. Rahman wanted to get back here for the Eid festival, so he forced Shankar to run the distance in just three days."

"Three days!" Dr. Sarma bellowed. "One hundred miles is almost double the distance an elephant can safely cover in that amount of time. The *mahout* should have known better. A journey like that could kill an elephant."

Mr. Choudhury was silent for a moment. When he spoke again, he sounded worried. "Is there anything you can do? Can you come help him?"

Dr. Sarma asked where they lived and learned they were in Lanka, ninety miles away from where he was now. The town was nowhere near the next camp he was scheduled to visit, but if he didn't go, who would tend to the *makhna*?

"I'm on my way," he said, as he'd replied so many other times.

∿

When Dr. Sarma arrived in Lanka, he found the Choudhury family looking handsome in newly purchased outfits. They were Muslim, and it was a custom on the festival of Eid to buy new clothes, go to the mosque, pray, and end the day with a big feast. It was clear that their day wasn't going exactly as planned, however.

Dr. Sarma greeted Mr. Choudhury and then asked to meet Rahman so he could learn more about Shankar's condition.

Mr. Choudhury brought Dr. Sarma to an orchard by a small creek where Rahman waited for them. Unlike the Choudhurys, Rahman wasn't wearing new clothes. Dr. Sarma took in the young man's T-shirt, the tears in the knees of his pants, the dirt beneath his fingernails. Although he was furious at Rahman for what he'd done to Shankar, he knew that since commercial logging in

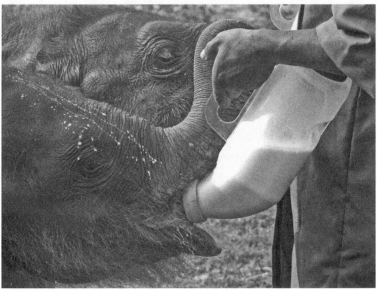

Asian elephant twins are rare, and feeding them is messy.

government owned forests in northeastern India had been banned, fewer people could afford to own elephants and fewer people became *mahouts*. Fewer *mahouts* meant much of their traditional knowledge about elephant care had been lost. It also meant that *mahouts* were often poorly paid and received little training. He felt sorry for Rahman, but still, he should've known better! Shankar had been entrusted to his care.

These thoughts swirled through Dr. Sarma's mind, but he had to focus. He pushed them away and asked Rahman to describe Shankar's symptoms.

"He hasn't been able to go to the bathroom since we returned from our trip," he said in a small voice.

Dr. Sarma considered Rahman's words. If the *makhna* was unable to defecate, there was something wrong with his intestines. Intestinal problems in elephants could be serious. They could even be deadly. "Take me to see him right away."

The second he saw Shankar, Dr. Sarma's suspicion about the *makhna*'s condition was confirmed. The area around the elephant's eyes was brick red in color—a clue to the cause of his ailment. "I think it's severe colic due to colonic impaction," Dr. Sarma told the Choudhurys. He didn't tell them it was possible that the condition was much worse. It could be paralysis of the intestine. In that case, there wasn't much he could do.

More Muslim families in their new clothes now gathered to see if the doctor could help the *makhna*. He estimated there were 50 people crowded around to see what would become of Shankar. Dr. Sarma didn't think about his audience. His full attention was on saving the elephant's life.

If he couldn't unblock the *makhna's* intestines, Shankar would die.

"First I need to give him fluids," he told the Choudhurys, knowing that dehydration could also lead to the animal's death.

Because of the urgency of the situation and the large volume of fluid the elephant needed, Dr. Sarma injected the fluids and medicines intravenously, using the veins on the back of the elephant's ear.

The fluids were just part of the treatment, though. Since the elephant's intestines were blocked, Dr. Sarma would have to unblock them. He'd have to give the *makhna* an enema—meaning he'd have to manually inject seven to ten gallons of warm water mixed with a mild detergent into Shankar's rectum to loosen the blockage.

He slipped on his gloves, stepped onto the stool Rahman had placed behind Shankar, and inserted his hand. Using a pump, he released the water and detergent mix. Within a minute of treatment, he heard the elephant's gut start to rumble. The enema was working. The rumble quickly grew louder.

Before Dr. Sarma could remove his hand, Shankar's intestines unblocked. With a volcanic eruption, the enema fluid and what must have been thirty pounds of poop shot out of the elephant—all over Dr. Sarma. He'd saved the *makhna's* life, but now he was dripping from head to toe in the animal's waste!

The onlookers screamed, but Dr. Sarma remained calm. He removed his gloved hand from Shankar, looked from the relieved *makhna* to the surprised crowd, and with a huge smile said, "Today's my lucky day! It's the festival of Eid, and now you can get me new clothes! Please go to the market. I wear size 42."

∿∿

That night, after bathing and changing his clothes and treating a total of 28 elephants, Dr. Sarma was exhausted. But he had one more important thing to do. Though it was already getting dark, he drove an hour and a half to the town of Tezpur, where he bought twenty packets of Lactogen 2 infant formula. He then drove back to Satsimalu camp for his final task of the day.

As the night birds snatched insects from the air, the *mahouts* slept, and the Muslim families feasted at the mosque, Dr. Sarma fed a bottle to Alaka's baby and thought about how lucky he was to be of service to the elephants.

ƎN OLD FRIƎND
•
2016

In November 2016, one year after treating Shankar, Dr. Sarma received a call from Mrs. Suparna Ganguli, the founder of an animal welfare group in India. She told him the Jumbo Circus was performing in Gujarat and asked if he could come.

As one of just three people in all of India appointed by the Central Zoo Authority to serve on the Circus Elephant Evaluation Committee, Dr. Sarma's job was to inspect the country's circus elephants and make sure they were being properly cared for. Although the state of Gujarat was 1,500 miles away from Assam, Dr. Sarma agreed to go.

The next day he flew to Ahmedabad, the largest city in Gujarat, where Mrs. Ganguli met him. From the busy city, the pair traveled 100 miles in a hired taxi to the town of Himatnagar. An orchestra playing old Hindi film music announced the presence of the circus before the two arrived in the city garden where the performers and their animals were camped. As he listened to the songs, Dr. Sarma thought about the circus and the elephants they kept.

Although many animal welfare groups in India thought keeping elephants in circuses was cruel and should be stopped, Dr. Sarma worried that if circuses were banned from having elephants, those animals currently kept by them would have nowhere safe to live. There wasn't a single place in India equipped to care for an elephant for its entire life in a manner that satisfied him. Furthermore, the law already prohibited tigers, lions, and bears from being in circuses. Elephants were the only animal left to draw an audience. If the elephants were removed, it would mean nobody would come. Then what would happen to the hundreds of poor people who made a living with the circus? And why take such a step when there was nowhere else for those elephants to be?

"There are five elephants in this circus right now," Mrs. Ganguli said, interrupting his thoughts.

Dr. Sarma nodded and stepped out of the car. The city garden smelled of spicy street foods. Children laughed and shouted. Hindi pop music blared from speakers. Crowds of squawking birds clustered in trees lush with berries. Everyone around him seemed happy. As he followed Mrs. Ganguli to the *pilkhana*, or stables, where the elephants were housed, he wondered how they were doing and if they were being well looked after.

In Assam captive elephants led a more natural life than in other parts of the country. They were able to bathe in rivers and graze in forests, their chains preventing them from wandering away. In some forests where small herds of elephants lived together, only the matriarch's legs were hobbled, as a family group always stayed with the female elder and would never leave her side. Elephant care in other regions of India was different, and often not very good. In some places, the social animals lived in isolation. In other places, they were forced to stand all day on hard surfaces. These abuses infuriated Dr. Sarma. He hoped he'd find these elephants in better conditions.

When they reached the *pilkhana*, he took out his notebook to record the details of the elephants and their health. Before he even saw the animals, though, he had to investigate their living quarters.

He looked around and observed the trees shading the enclosure. He saw the piles of cut grass and fresh vegetation and the large bowls of water. Satisfied with what he saw, he stepped into the *pilkhana* to test the surface upon which the large animals stood, making sure it wasn't concrete that would hurt their feet while standing and hurt their joints while sleeping. The surface was soft and bedded over with straw. Finally, he walked the perimeter of the *pilkhana* to ensure there was adequate drainage and that the area was clean—no dung or left-over food to rot.

"It looks good," he told Mrs. Ganguli, recording these observations in his notebook. "Is there any other live-stock in the area?" he then asked, making sure the ele-phants wouldn't come into contact with any cattle-borne diseases.

"I don't know," Mrs. Ganguli said. "I'll go talk to the circus manager and find out."

Mrs. Ganguli left, and a *mahout* brought Dr. Sarma his first elephant to examine. The elephant was a beautiful and regal-looking cow with lightly freckled skin around her trunk, eyes, and the folds of her ears. He read her body language to see if she was ready to be approached. She looked relaxed, so he stepped closer and said hello.

"My name is KK," he said, introducing himself, as he always did when tending to an elephant he hadn't met before.

The elephant responded to his greeting with a flap of her ears. "I'm guessing you're about 40," he said, using the flapping to help him detect her age. Older elephants have harder ear cartilage and therefore the flapping sound is louder than in younger animals.

She made a soft grunting sound—and then investi-gated his pockets.

As Dr. Sarma reached into his bag for the treat he carried, she opened her mouth wide with the hopes of something big and juicy. Dr. Sarma brought out a sweet, ripe pineapple.

Once she swallowed the tasty snack, Dr. Sarma began his examination. As he always did when inspecting an elephant, he observed all of her systems, searching for signs of illness. The elephant swayed and flapped her ears, chirping and rumbling, as he inspected her.

As Dr. Sarma was checking the elephant's heart rate, Mrs. Ganguli returned and told him that there were no cattle on the circus grounds. Dr. Sarma thanked her, then continued his examination. It was time to look at the elephant's feet. He perched on a stool in front of her and gave her a command to raise her foot. She readily granted the request. Dr. Sarma smiled at her gentle demeanor.

He'd just started checking her front right foot for overgrown toenails when his phone rang. A man from the World Wide Fund for Nature in Assam was calling to ask Dr. Sarma for advice about an injured *koonkie* he'd been using to drive away a herd of wild elephants from some rice fields. Dr. Sarma was speaking in Assamese, giving the man advice and telling him he'd come check on the elephant as soon as he returned, when he felt the elephant that he was examining step forward and wrap her trunk around his shoulders.

"Be careful!" Mrs. Ganguli shouted. "She's going to hurt you!"

Dr. Sarma held up his hand, indicating for Mrs. Ganguli to stay calm, and studied the elephant. Her touch was gentle, he felt, more a show of love than an act of aggression. It was as if she knew him somehow, as if she understood the language he'd been speaking—as if they were friends.

Dr. Sarma didn't move. Why was she touching him like this? Did she understand that he was there to look after her well-being? Sure, elephants often touched him and inspected his pockets, but never before had one hugged him, which it seemed she was doing.

Dr. Sarma gently unwound her trunk from his neck and looked at her. He studied the browns and grays of her skin. He gazed at her pink speckled ears. He looked into her eye and thought about all the elephants he'd known over the years. They were all special, but there was something different about this elephant, something he couldn't place. He wanted to know more about her.

"I'll be right back," he said to both the elephant and Mrs. Ganguli. He rose from his stool, stepped out of the *pilkhana*, and walked to the small trailer that housed the circus manager.

"I need to see the records for the old female elephant," he said when the manager appeared. "I have some questions." He didn't say what his questions were. He wasn't even sure he knew. He just had a feeling.

The manager invited him into the trailer as he searched through the files on his desk. Finally, he handed Dr. Sarma a paper. "I think this is what you're looking for."

Dr. Sarma thanked him and sat down to read the documents that recorded the history of the elephant's life before coming to the circus. The first thing he learned was the elephant's name.

"Lokhimai," he said to himself, his breath quickening. Could she be the same Lokhimai whom he'd loved all those years ago? It was too much to hope for. Lokhimai was a typical Assamese name. It was unlikely she was the same elephant—unlikely, but not impossible. He read on.

Next he learned that Lokhimai had been treated some fourteen years ago for a severe abscess on her back. Now Dr. Sarma felt his heart hammering as he considered the possibility that she truly was the same elephant. If so, had she recognized him?

As he read the rest of the records, he learned that Lokhimai had been sold at the *mela*, a Sanskrit word meaning a gathering or a fair, in the city of Sonpur in the state of Bihar. A man named Amir Hussein from Dipila had sold her.

Dr. Sarma dropped the paper, hardly believing what he'd read. Amir Hussein had been Lokhimai's owner. Was his feeling that he knew this elephant true? Could Lokhimai be his dear friend from all those years ago? Had she heard his voice, heard the soft Assamese language and recalled the sweet days in Assam with the people who loved her before she'd been a circus elephant? Had she remembered the doctor who'd cared for her?

Then he recalled something else. Dr. Sarma jumped up from his seat and rushed back outside.

Love for each other.

"Her feet! I have to check her toenails," he shouted to a surprised Mrs. Ganguli. He stepped into the *pilkhana* and immediately went to check for the unusual number of toenails on Lokhimai's hind left foot.

"Three toenails!" Dr. Sarma exclaimed, trembling with emotion. *"Boith,"* he then said, giving Lokhimai the command to kneel. The elephant bent her legs, and Dr. Sarma looked at her back. He saw the huge white scar where fourteen years ago he'd removed the large piece of skin to cure her abscess. Dr. Sarma circled back to Lokhimai's head and touched the side of her face. "It's you, my old friend, isn't it?" he said, his eyes filling with tears.

As if in answer to his question, Lokhimai again circled Dr. Sarma with her trunk. The elephant doctor put his face against her lower jaw and wept. He wept at being reunited with his old friend. He wept for his love of elephants. He wept because Lokhimai recognized and remembered him. Most of all he wept because her greeting was a display of the amazing emotions and memory of the most magnificent and extraordinary of creatures.

Dr. Sarma had been helping elephants for nearly thirty years, and on that day he felt that they cared about him as much as he cared about them.

He had no doubt that this was love.

SAVING ELEPHANTS

*"It is the greatest of all mistakes to do nothing
because you can only do little."*
—Sydney Smith

a beaver builds a dam, holding back water and creating a pond and restoring or maintaining a wetland. A wolf pack brings down a deer or an elk, keeping the prey in check so that the herbivores don't overgraze and eat all the plants. A woodpecker creates nesting holes other birds depend on. Otters eat the sea urchins that would destroy the kelp. These animals all have one thing in common: they're keystone species, helping to create and maintain an entire ecosystem. If a keystone species were to disappear, there wouldn't be another species that could take its job or fill its niche.

Like the animals above (and there are many more examples, fungi and plants included), elephants are a keystone species. Both African and Asian elephants play an important role in maintaining the ecosystems in which they live. Asian elephants do this in several ways. First, when they eat they create gaps in the vegetation. These gaps let the sun reach the forest floor and allow new plants to grow. Second, they're a major source of seed dispersal. How? Through their poop.

Elephants are also an umbrella species. Like an umbrella that protects those beneath it, an umbrella species protects other animals. But in this case, the importance of an umbrella species has to do with its range. If an animal with a large habitat requirement is protected, so are all the other animals that share that habitat.

Think, for example, about the farmers who are making elephant-friendly tea farms. Say a bunch of these farmers got together and formed a corridor of habitat that allowed elephants to move, unharmed, from one farm to another. In this case, they'd be offering protection not just to elephants but to all the animals that share that habitat.

Besides the role they play in ecology, elephants are amazing in their own right. They're intelligent and empathetic, emotional and social. But sadly, as you've learned in this book, their habitat is shrinking. Like so many other animals across the globe, elephants are disappearing. It's up to us to save them.

Of course, most of us don't live with elephants, so it

might be hard to think of how to protect them when they're so far away. We might not live with elephants, but we all live with wild animals. We live with spiders, ants, birds, squirrels, mice, lizards, snakes, bees, and many other creatures.

So, what does living with a spider or a bee have to do with living with an elephant?

Think of conservation like a spiral. The center of the spiral, the nucleus, is the part closest to you—your backyard or apartment balcony, for example. The nucleus is the place you can most directly influence. You can grow native plants for local pollinators and other wildlife. You can provide food and water for the birds. You can keep your house cat inside. You can opt not to use chemical pesticides. And you can reduce your ecological footprint by buying less stuff, especially stuff like plastic that doesn't break down and quickly ends up in the trash.

As the spiral unwinds, you move away from the nucleus and travel a little farther from your home. You're now in your hometown. Here you have less direct control, but you can still have an impact and a voice. You can find out who your city leaders are and learn what they stand for. Then you can educate your parents about who you think they should vote for and why. You can also find out about local environmental policies. For example, does your city recycle? Do they use chemicals in the parks that could harm wildlife? Can you adopt a park or neighborhood and make sure it's clean? What about planting trees or getting a compost pile or garden started at your school?

Journeying outward in the spiral, you arrive at the state and then the region—the Southwest or Northeast, for example. What are the state and regional environmental issues? Are there endangered species in your region? If so, what are the issues affecting their conservation? Who are the major players, the people who could significantly affect the situation? Listen to and learn about all sides. Remember, knowledge is power. The more you know, the more you can speak up for what you believe.

The spiral reaches its outer layers as you leave the state, first leading to the country and eventually to the whole world. For many, this is where elephants come in. Although you might not go to India and directly save an elephant, there are other ways you can help protect them and other endangered species around the world. Being a smart consumer is one way. For example, in this book you learned that most of the world's black tea comes from Assam, and that to grow the tea the forests are cut down and converted into plantations. Lisa Mills, a wildlife conservation outreach specialist at the University of Montana who first introduced me to Dr. Sarma, and Julie Stein of Wildlife Friendly Enterprise Network are working with tea growers to encourage their support of conservation and safe passage of Asian elephants as they move through tea plantations in India. You can learn about Certified Elephant Friendly tea at www .elephantfriendlytea.wordpress.com and support elephant conservation—one cup of tea at a time.

It's not just what we consume that helps protect species. Conservation also requires speaking up. It's having a voice and educating others. It's reducing our ecological footprint. It's supporting the environmental groups and local people doing the work you believe in, and maybe it's even the career you chose. You can be a veterinarian, like Dr. Sarma, or a teacher, an environmental educator, an artist, a policy maker. . . .

Whatever you do, you can help spread the word that the time to act for elephants, and for every other species—including us—is now!

You matter.

Your voice matters.

So spread the word and ask others to do the same.

a LETTER FROM DR. SARMA

My young friends, greetings from the land of elephants! For the past 30 years I have followed my passion and worked with the largest animals on land. My love of elephants began with my childhood friendship with Lakshmi, a noble old-lady elephant who for a time lived with my family in our small village in northeastern India in the state of Assam.

In the years since then, the adoring looks and gentle touches of my elephant patients have turned me into more than just a professional vet. I deeply love the species, and after so many years of working with them, I can declare that I represent the elephants. There are no other veterinary subjects that are as sensitive, expressive, and cooperative as elephants are. Though I am

Dr. Sarma in action.

small and they are immense, they accept me. Most of them not only recognize me from my physical appearance but from my voice as well.

Elephants are a measure of a healthy and green earth. They enrich the forest with biomass, and they ensure regeneration of the forest by seed dispersal. They teach us about the remedies available in naturally growing herbs. Now scientists have even discovered that the P_{53} gene of the elephant may help us cure cancer.

Elephants have been an important part of Indian culture, and especially our culture in Assam. Today in Assam we have 10 percent of the world's remaining wild Asian elephants and about 1,200 captive ones. We also have a huge human population. It is not always easy for people and elephants to coexist.

Because I have been blessed with a strong body and a sense of adventure, I have been able to help and save many elephants that have come into conflict with people. But it is up to all of us humans, the elephants' friends throughout the ages, to take decisive steps to ensure their preservation. I have one message for you: love elephants, love soil, love water, love air—love the blue planet—love our mother earth!

—KK Sarma

aUTHOR'S NOTe

I first met Dr. Sarma in April 2015 when he came to the United States and Lisa Mills invited me to hear him speak at the veterinary school at North Carolina State University. He was gracious, smart, funny, warm, and passionate, and I spent many hours asking him about his life with elephants. I learned much in those two days, but I wanted to learn more. To do so, I knew I had to go to India.

Seeing how enthusiastic I was, Dr. Sarma invited me to come visit him. The following October, Lisa Mills was heading to Assam to work on her elephant conservation projects. The timing was perfect. My husband and I decided to go with her. In October 2015 we boarded a plane for the two-day journey to northeastern India, where we would spend three weeks with Dr. Sarma.

He took us with him to his elephant health-care clinics, and where we got to see him in action. We traveled with him to national parks and tea plantations (where I saw a herd of over 200 wild elephants). It was an amazing experience. The whole time I was there I took notes and asked questions.

I was sad to leave, wondering when I'd see Dr. Sarma again. Then, in the winter of 2017, he had a chance to visit me in the United States. During this time he spoke to schoolchildren and community groups about his work with elephants. I spent many more hours interviewing him and asking questions about his life. His energy and enthusiasm are endless; his heart is large. I am so grateful that he entrusted me with his stories, and I hope that in writing this book about his life I can also help spread the word about the plight of elephants.

As for Dr. Sarma, he continues his effort to rescue rogues, care for captive elephants, and come to the aid of wild ones. As of 2020, he has saved 139 *musth* bulls and hundreds of people. Of his work, he says, "What elephants have done for me I could not repay in ten lifetimes. My heart is with the forest, with the land, with the people, and most of all with the elephants. Without the elephants, I am nobody."

Facts about Asian Elephants

Class: Mammalia
Order: Proboscidea
Family: Elephantidae
Genus and Species: *Elephas maximus*

- Asian elephants are in both a different species and a different genus than African elephants. Asian elephants are *Elephas maximus* and African elephants are *Loxodonta africana*. The two cannot breed and produce fertile offspring. Additionally, Asian elephants are smaller than African elephants, have smaller ears, a more convex (hunched) back, and smoother skin.

- There are approximately 50,000 Asian elephants remaining in India, Nepal, Bhutan, Bangladesh, Sri Lanka, Myanmar, Thailand, Laos, Cambodia, Vietnam, China, Malaysia, and Indonesia. They were once found all the way from Syria to northern China.
- With 27,000 wild elephants, India has the largest population in Asia, and with 5,500 wild elephants, Assam has the largest population in India.
- Asian elephants are officially listed as an endangered species by the US Fish and Wildlife Service (USFW) and by the International Union for the Conservation of Nature (IUCN).
- More than two thirds of an Asian elephant's day may be spent feeding on grasses, tree bark, roots, leaves, and small stems, as well as cultivated crops such as rice, sugarcane, and bananas. Asian elephants do not sleep much, and they roam over great distances while foraging for the large quantities of food they require to sustain their massive bodies.
- Asian elephants can produce about 220 pounds of dung per day, which helps to disperse germinating seeds.
- Asian elephants weigh from 6,000 to 14,000 pounds and are 7 to 12 feet tall.
- Asian elephants can detect sound as low as 8 hertz and as high as 12,000 hertz. (A hertz is a unit of frequency.) They can use infrasonic sound—sound emitted below the human range of hearing—to communicate with other elephants up to several

miles away. Part of this communication is sent through the ground and picked up with their feet.

- Asian elephants have an amazing sense of smell and are very tactile, relying on touch in all forms of behavior, from parenting to defense to exploration. The trunk, which is actually a fusion of the upper lip and long nose, is the most tactile part of the elephant's body; it is used to stroke, touch, explore, caress, reassure, take in water, breathe, and make sounds, among other things. With about 40,000 muscles in its trunk, an Asian elephant can lift as much as 600 pounds or pick up an object as small as a coin. Asian elephants have one small projection at the end of their trunk, called a finger, which they use for picking up objects.

- Female Asian elephants don't have tusks, and some males don't either. Those males that do have tusks are called tuskers, and those that don't are called *makhnas*. Females and some *makhnas* have tushes in place of tusks. Tushes are long teeth that are hidden by their lips. Tusks and tushes are actually an elephant's upper incisor teeth.

- Elephants go through six sets of molar teeth in a lifetime. Dental health is essential to their overall health. Once the last set of molar teeth is all worn out, an elephant can no longer chew properly and will die.

- An Asian elephant's skin may lack pigment in the ears, trunk, or neck and show pinkish spots for this reason. Additionally, they have sparse sweat glands and therefore can't tolerate heat.

- Asian elephants are extremely sociable, forming groups of six to seven related females led by the oldest female, the matriarch. These groups occasionally join others to form herds.
- Asian elephants can recognize hundreds of individuals, and they exhibit a wide variety of behaviors associated with grief, mourning, learning, mimicry, play, compassion, cooperation, and memory. All the females in a herd take part in caring for the young.
- At 19–22 months, an elephant's pregnancy is the longest of any mammal. A newborn calf weighs about 220 pounds and stands about three feet. Cows usually give birth to one calf every two to four years.
- Asian elephants live to be about 60 in the wild and about 80 in captivity.
- Starting sometime between ages 15 and 20, bull elephants yearly go into a normal and temporary condition called *musth,* which increases their testosterone as much as 60 times higher than in a non-*musth* period. Only a few bulls in an area go into *musth* at a time. The *musth* period lasts for several months and causes males to become very aggressive.

GLOSSARY

Adivasi: An umbrella term for a diverse set of 96 ethnic and tribal groups considered to be the aboriginal people of India. The British later enslaved them and brought them to Assam from the Central Indian states of Bihar, Orissa, Bengal, and Madhya Pradesh to work the tea plantations. Today they are also known as tea tribes or laborers.

Ayurvedic: One of the world's oldest holistic, or whole-body, healing approaches. This system was developed in India more than 3,000 years ago. Ayurvedic healing is based on the belief that health is a balance between the mind, body, and spirit.

Assam tea: A black tea grown in Assam India that comes from the plant *Camellia sinensis* variety *assamica.* Assam teas, which are often made into breakfast blend teas, are grown in the lowland regions of Assam where there is a cool, arid winter and a hot, humid rainy season. Assam is one of the largest tea-producing regions in the world, and each year the tea estates there collectively harvest approximately 1,500 million pounds of tea.

Bodo: A tribal group of people living in northeastern India, primarily in Assam, and the largest tribal group in the region. The Bodos were the earliest settlers in Assam.

Brahmin: The highest of the four traditional castes, or *varna*—social classes passed down through family—in Hinduism. Brahmins are often priests and teachers.

dhoti: A rectangular piece of unstitched cloth, usually about 15 feet long, that is worn wrapped around the waist, tucked between the legs and then tucked into the fabric at the back of the waist. Typically a dhoti hangs to mid-calf. Dhotis are worn mostly by men.

Eid: Also known as Eid al-Fitr, Eid is a religious holiday celebrated by Muslims around the world that marks the end of the monthlong daily fasting of Ramadan. It is known as the "festival of breaking fast."

gamosa: An article of clothing that is worn like a scarf by men and women throughout Assam. The gamosa is woven out of white thread with intricate red inlays. Similar to a towel, it is rectangular in shape, around two feet in width and four feet in length.

Ganesha: Lord Ganesha, or Ganesh, is a Hindu god recognized around the world for his elephant head. Ganesha is the Lord of Good Fortune who provides prosperity, fortune and success. He is also the Lord of Beginnings and the Remover of Obstacles.

Hinduism: An ancient religion or way of life practiced primarily in India and Nepal. There are an estimated 1 billion people who practice Hinduism, and about 80 percent of India's population regard themselves as Hindus. The word *Hindu* comes from the Sanskrit word *sindhu*, which means "river" and refers to the Indus Valley. Hindus have many gods, one of which is Lord Ganesha, the elephant-headed god. The earliest Hindu texts, the Vedas, are estimated to date back as early as 1500 BCE.

koonkie: A captive elephant used for work. In Assam people have been using trained elephants for thousands of years. Today, *koonkies* in Assam are primarily used for antipoaching patrols and for driving back herds of wild elephants from farmers' lands, but they are also used for tourism. People started taming Asian elephants for work more than 4,000 years ago.

lungi: A skirt-like garment that is wrapped around the waist and extends to the ankle. Lungis are worn by both men and women across Southeast Asia and especially in India.

mahout: A trained elephant handler, keeper, and trainer.

makhna: A male Asian elephant without tusks.

megaherbivore: An animal, such as an elephant, that weighs over 2,000 pounds and is an herbivore, meaning it eats only plants.

mela: A Sanskrit word meaning "gathering," "festival," or "to meet." In India, a mela can be a religious, cultural, commercial, or sport-related event.

musth: A periodic and temporary condition when a bull elephant has a rise in the reproductive hormone testosterone. This increase makes a bull aggressive and ready to challenge other bulls for females. *Musth* comes from the Hindi word meaning "intoxicated."

matriarch: The oldest and largest female elephant that leads her herd. In a crisis, the herd will rely on the matriarch to make the major decisions. Her memory of food and water sources may be the key to survival during difficult times. Successful matriarchs earn respect through their wisdom, confidence, and connections with other elephants. As they travel, her daughters and their calves follow the lead of the matriarch elephant, walking behind her in single file. The matriarch teaches her daughters how to care for their own young.

namaskar: A traditional Indian greeting or show of respect made by holding the palms together in front of the face or chest and slightly bowing the head.

pheromone: A chemical that is secreted and causes a response in other members of the same species. There are pheromones in *musth* fluid that bring a female elephant of mating age into a *musth* bull's vicinity.

Republic Day: A national holiday in India celebrated each year on January 26 to honor the date in 1950 when the Indian constitution was signed and India became a republic.

Singpho: A widespread people group living in Burma, China, and India. In India they primarily live in the state of Arunachal Pradesh and Assam. The Singpho are divided into clans known as Gams, each led by a chief. The Singpho were the first people to drink what is now known as Assam tea.

temporin: A thick, tarry secretion that comes out of glands on the side of a male elephant's face during *musth*. The temporin, also known in Assam as *kamsindur*, trickles down into the elephant's mouth and causes the glands to swell and press on his eyes, both of which cause the elephant great discomfort. The fluid has a strong smell and has falsely been called "elephant's tears." Some people believe that if you rub a little bit of this secretion on the object of your affection, you will win his or her heart.

tush: A tusklike tooth found in female Asian elephants and some *makhnas*. Tushes seldom extend more than a few inches past the lip line and are slightly different than tusks. Tushes are small and brittle, which causes them to break easily.

tusker: A male Asian elephant that has tusks. The percentage of males with tusks varies by region.

Approximately 90 percent of male elephants in India had tusks, but because of selective ivory poaching, starting largely in the 1970s, this number is changing. According to population estimates gathered by the Assam forest department, the percentage of *makhnas* in Assam increased from 62 to 76 percent in Assam between 1993 and 2008.